5

The Weird and the Beautiful

Books by RICHARD HEADSTROM

The Beetles of America
Spiders of the United States
Your Insect Pet
Frogs, Toads, and Salamanders as Pets
Whose Track Is It?
Lizards as Pets
A Complete Guide to Nests in the United States
Nature in Miniature
Adventures with Freshwater Animals
Adventures with Insects
Adventures with a Hand Lens
Garden Friends and Foes
Birds' Nests of the West
Birds' Nests
The Living Year
Adventures with a Microscope
The Story of Russia
The Origin of Man
Families of Flowering Plants
Lobsters, Crabs, and Their Relatives
Your Reptile Pet

The Weird
and the
Beautiful

The Story of the Portuguese Man-of-War,
the Sailors-by-the-Wind,
and Their Exotic Relatives of the Deep

Richard Headstrom

Illustrated by the author

New York • *Cornwall Books* • London

© 1984 by Rosemont Publishing and Printing Corporation

Cornwall Books
440 Forsgate Drive
Cranbury, NJ 08512

Cornwall Books
25 Sicilian Avenue
London WC1A 2QH, England

Cornwall Books
2133 Royal Windsor Drive
Unit 1
Mississauga, Ontario
Canada L5J 1K5

Library of Congress Cataloging in Publication Data

Headstrom, Birger Richard, 1902–
    The weird and the beautiful.

    Bibliography: p.
    Includes index.
    1.   Coelenterata.   I.   Title.
QL375.H4   593'.5   81-67780
ISBN 0-8453-4727-6

To my wife

Printed in the United States of America

Contents

Preface

"I saw in 1590, lying with a fleet of her majesties ships about the islands in the Azores, almost six months, the greatest part of the time we were becalmed, all the sea so replenished with several sorts of jellies, and forms of serpents, adders, snakes as seemed wonderful; some green, some black, some yellow, some white, some of diverse colors; and many of them had life, and some there were a yard and a half, and two yards long; which had I not seen, I could hardly have believed. A man could not draw a bucket of water clear of such life."

So wrote Sir Richard Hawkins, an Elizabethan sea captain and perhaps the first Englishman to do so, about the most weird and most beautiful animals to be found in the animal kingdom. Few people have seen these animals alive although they occur in countless numbers in the sea. We know some of them as jellyfishes, others as corals. Everyone who has taken a high school or college biology course is familiar with the freshwater representative, the hydra. But probably few of such students have ever seen a living hydra, though the animal is common in practically every pond, stream, or lake.

The jellyfishes, corals, hydras and others—such as the sea anemones, sea pens, sea feathers, and sea fans—comprise a colorful, interesting, and important group of animals. A brief account of them may be found in most books on natural history and in college texts on zoology, but few, if any, books have been written exclusively about them. The author feels there is a need for such a book, and hence has prepared the present volume for the general reader as a brief introduction to these fascinating and exotic animals.

Portuguese Man-of-War, **Physalia pelagica**

1. The Portuguese Man-of-War

Anyone who has seen a flotilla of Portuguese Men-of-War sailing on a tropic sea is not likely to forget the sight for a long time, if ever. At a distance, as seen from the deck of a ship, the flotilla, moving over the surface of the calm sea, appears to be a profusion of colorful bubbles that, in the play of the sun's rays, often shine with a startling and beautiful iridescence. Then, as the ship approaches, the flotilla may suddenly descend beneath the surface and disappear from view, perhaps to rise and reappear at a later time.

The most conspicuous feature of the Portuguese Man-of-War or *Physalia pelagica*, to give the animal its scientific name (from the Greek words for "bladder" and "sea," respectively), is the float, an oblong, pear-shaped bladder or sac formed of a delicate, translucent membrane, brilliantly tinted with colors that may range from a deep ruby red to a brilliant blue, or from red to green. The upper part of the float consists of a series of bubble-like chambers surmounted by a longitudinal red crest or sail running lengthwise along the float, which may be as much as fourteen inches in length. The float is filled with a self-generated gas which the dreadnought can inflate or deflate at will. Thus it is able to seek various depths of the sea as the occasion may require. On the surface, however, the Portuguese Man-of-War is a captive of the wind and must sail in whatever direction the wind propels it.

From the underside of the float extend or depend long, ribbonlike streamers or tentacles. At this point it must be explained that the Portuguese Man-of-War is not a single animal, but is composed of a number of individual animals called zooids in what is commonly called a colony, the individual animals separately performing various functions and thus exhibiting what is known as division of labor. All these individual animals communicate with each other through connecting tubes, so that those whose function is to gather food may pass it along to those performing some other function. Thus beneath the float are zooids concerned with capturing prey, others with flask-shaped bodies that consume the prey and pass the food along to the others, these feeding zooids being a brilliant blue in color and each with a terminal mouth and with one or more tentacles, and still others that look like bunches of grapes and are a salmon-pink in color. These latter are the reproductive zooids and are responsible for the perpetuation of the species.

Some of the tentacles are quite short, but others are much longer and can stretch out, retract, and coil up like a wire spring; thus they can, on windy days, be extended as much as forty to fifty feet into the depths of the sea to act as a drag-anchor to keep the float from being too swiftly blown before the wind. Situated along the tentacles are microscopic stinging or nettling cells, explosive structures that secrete a virulent poison as deadly as cobra venom. It is with these tentacles and stinging cells that the Portuguese Man-of-War captures its prey. Fishes of considerable size are completely paralyzed and are then drawn up by the contracting tentacles to the multitudinous mouths of the feeding zooids, which suck them dry. It is an awesome sight to observe a fish being caught by the Man-of-War and then carried slowly upward to be devoured by it. Although it may seem surprising, one little species of fish (*Nomeus gronovii*) swims freely among the tentacles without being affected by them, the *Physalia* apparently tolerating their presence. Here is an illustration of what is known as symbiosis, a partnership between two unrelated species for their mutual benefit. The small fish seemingly serve as a lure, tempting other fishes within reach of the tentacles and thus providing more food for the *Physalia*, which in return for such service protects *Nomeus* from its enemies. Doubtless *Nomeus* also dines on the scraps of food left by its protector, which probably captures more food than it can consume.

A swimmer coming in contact with only a single tentacle of the Portuguese Man-of-War can sustain a severe injury and may suffer indescribable agony. A sting from the animal produces a burning, irritating sensation, and in some cases cramps, nausea, and a difficulty in breathing. First aid treatment consists of bathing the affected part with alcohol, lighter fluid, or some other organic solvent, after which a doctor should be sought as soon as possible.

The Portuguese Men-of-War are often carried north by the Gulf Stream, and quite frequently hundreds of the animals are washed ashore along the Atlantic coast of the United States. Sometimes the beaches of Florida may be covered with them. The gas-filled balloons quickly dry up in the sun and if then stepped upon explode with a loud pop, a source of amusement for young boys and also for those not so young. One must be careful not to step on the tentacles, however, since they retain their nettling properties long after the animals are dead.

2. The Sailors-by-the-Wind

Closely related to the Portuguese Man-of-War are entrancing creatures known as Sailors-by-the-Wind, a name given them by the Elizabethan mariners who were also responsible for naming the Portuguese Man-of-War. Seen at a distance from the deck of a sailing vessel, they may often be found covering the ocean as far as the eye can see, each a little blue boat. No wonder they have captured man's imagination as no other animals have done.

A common species occurring in southern waters and often borne northward by the Gulf Stream is *Velella mutica*, the name *Velella* meaning little sail. It has a disc-like, rectangular bladder-like float four to five inches long, which is divided into a number of concentric, communicating compartments, with a triangular sail or keel-like crest that extends diagonally across the top. Extending down beneath its center is a single trunk which is a feeding zooid bearing the principal mouth and stomach of the colony, for, like the Portuguese Man-of-War, the Sailors-by-the-Wind are colonial animals. Surrounding the trunk are small reproductive individuals or zooids, which bear the reproductive organs; surrounding them and projecting from the outer edge of the float is a series of numerous, long, bright blue tentacles armed with stinging cells. The float is of an exquisite deep blue-green color, and when myriads of them are seen on a calm sea in bright sunlight the effect is most spectacular. Like the Portuguese Man-of-War, *Velella* is a captive of the wind. When the wind blows and catches its "sail" *Velella* moves through the water just like a ship sailing before the wind. A related species, *Velella luta*, is found in the Pacific Ocean from Vancouver to Mexico.

Often associated with *Velella* is *Porpita linneana* which differs from *Velella* in that it has no sail. Its disc-like float is flat and circular, about an inch in diameter, and a bright blue, shading into a beautiful iridescence in the center, and is surrounded on all sides by a radiating series of zooids. Some of them are reproductive in function while others perform tactile and protective services. *Porpita* is found along the South Atlantic coast and is often seen in such numbers from a ship crossing the Gulf Stream that the ocean for miles appears to be flecked with specks of blue, a scene of such beauty as to enthrall the spectator.

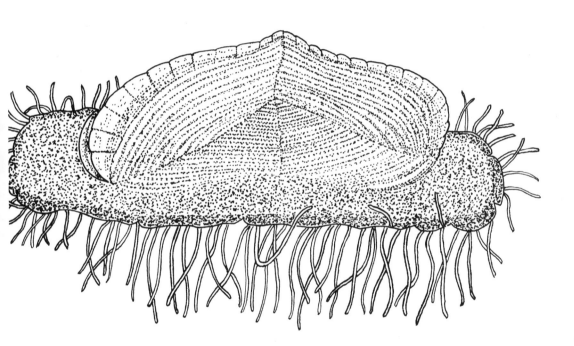

Sailors-by-the-Wind, **Velella mutica**

3. The Siphonophores

The Portuguese Man-of-War and the Sailors-by-the-Wind are known as siphonophores, free-floating communities or colonies of individual animals (zooids) which are specialized for different functions, their structures varying according to the function they perform. Such colonies are termed polymorphic. The members of the colony exhibit a division of labor similar to that of the various organs found in the body of higher animals. Thus, digestion is carried on by digestive zooids, reproduction by reproductive zooids (of two sexes), swimming by special swimming zooids, and so on. As has already been mentioned, all the zooids or individual animals are in communication with each other by means of connecting tubes, so that the food of the feeding zooids may be passed along to those that perform in a different function.

In the siphonophores, two general types of structure may be observed. In one type the individual members bud off from a long axial tube, the upper end of which is expanded to form a float filled with air or gas which serves to keep the colony right side up in the water. In the other type, such an axial tube is absent, the various individuals budding off from the lower side of an enormously enlarged float. Most of the siphonophores are of the first type.

In this more common type, the individuals that bud off from the axial tube immediately beneath the float are free-swimming zooids that are present in pairs. Beneath these, at intervals on the axis, are groups of individuals or zooids, each group consisting of the bract, a flat, scale-like

16

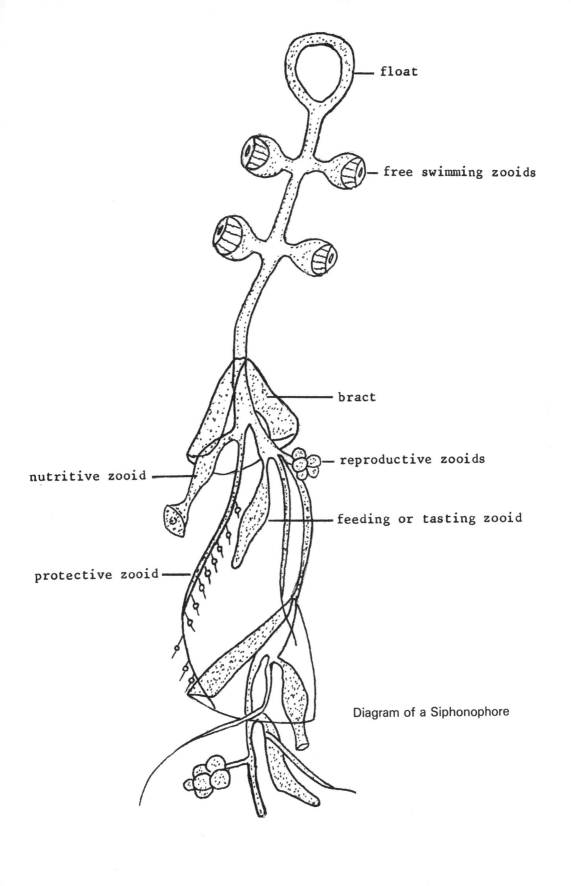

float

free swimming zooids

bract

reproductive zooids

nutritive zooid

feeding or tasting zooid

protective zooid

Diagram of a Siphonophore

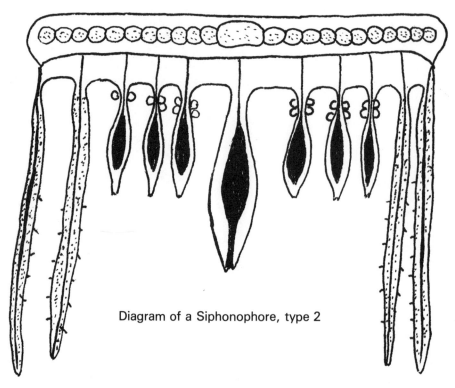

Diagram of a Siphonophore, type 2

protective zooid; a nutritive zooid, which is the mouth and stomach of the colony; a protective zooid furnished with a long tentacle and stinging cells; a club-shaped palp, which is apparently a feeling or tasting zooid; and finally the reproductive zooids, which are usually unisexual, that is, either male or female. A colony of this kind floats or swims slowly about in the sea. In some instances, the colonies may be many feet in length and contain many thousands of individuals. Hence the siphonophores are essentially pelagic animals (living in the open sea), though some forms occur in deep water, and are generally found in the warmer seas where they are among the most beautiful and conspicuous animals of the marine ecosystem. The siphonophores number about 250 species.

A siphonophore rather common along the New England coast is the species *Cupulita cara*. The members of the colony are arranged along the axial tube, at the top of which is the comparatively small float, an elliptical cavity containing a bubble of an oily substance. Below the float are four to six swimming zooids, in two longitudinal rows, whose function is to provide locomotion for the colony. Beneath the swimming zooids are

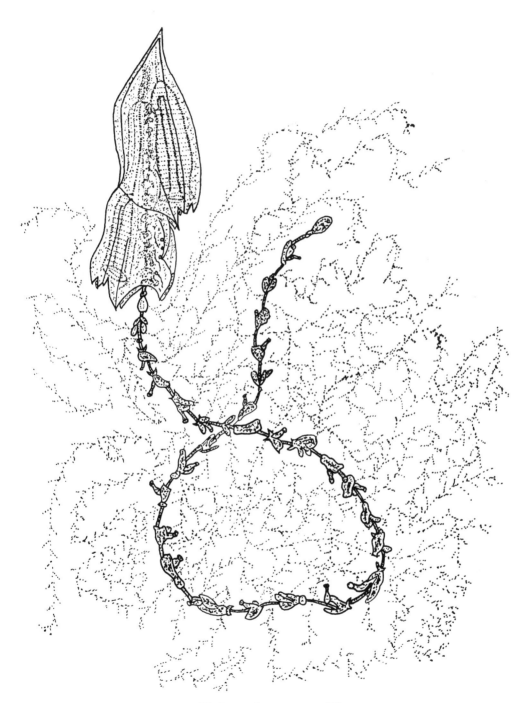

Diphyopsis campanulifera

successive similar groups of zooids, each group containing usually a protective bract, a palp, a feeling zooid with a tentacle, and a reproductive zooid. In describing the coloration of the colony, Alexander Agassiz, the naturalist and oceanographer, writes: "The float is a brilliant garnet color; from it hangs the rosy-colored axis, with its pale swimming bells (the swimming zooids), and farther down, the scale, protecting the different kinds of feeding polyps (zooids), with their various kinds of tentacles projecting in all sorts of angles and curves from the main axis of the body, like the festoons of a chandelier; the darker colored polyps, tipped and mottled with scarlet, being visible underneath the protecting scales."

One of the more beautiful of the siphonophores is the species *Diphyopsis campanulifera*. This colony does not have a float, the group of zooids being suspended instead from the two swimming zooids, which are

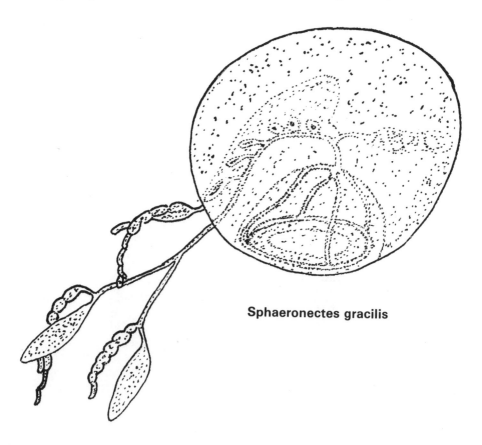

Sphaeronectes gracilis

angular, tapered, and of somewhat the same size. They drive the colony forward and keep it on the surface. Between these two zooids, two wings have grown together to form a canal from which a slender tubule extends for a considerable distance into the water and to which are attached, at regular intervals, a number of groups of polymorphic zooids. There may be as many as ninety or more of these groups in large colonies, each group with a protective bract, which is something like a cape and encloses a feeding zooid, a tasting zooid, and a long, slender tentacle. This tentacle has numerous branches armed with powerful stinging cells that can kill the small animals on which the colony feeds. They are digested by the feeding zooids present in each group. *Campanulifera* lives in the open sea and may often be seen in the waters of the Gulf Stream.

In the species *Sphaeronectes gracilis* there is only one nectophore, as the swimming zooid is called. It is responsible for keeping the colony afloat and moving it through the water, although there is a rudiment of a float which may be seen through the thick gelatinous upper portion of the bell-shaped nectophore. From a pit in one side a stem, to which are attached the groups of polymorphic zooids, extends into the water. Each group consists of as feeding zooid, a fighting zooid, or tentacle provided with stinging cells, a reproductive zooid, and a swimming zooid. These groups eventually become detached, lead an independent life, and become sexually mature. They become, in other words, a reproductive generation. These groups are known individually as an eudoxia.

In zoological taxonomy, the siphonophores belong to a division (phylum) of the animal kingdom known as Coelenterata, or the coelenterates. Now just what are coelenterates?

4. The Coelenterates

The coelenterates were once called plants or plant-animals (zoophytes) because they look so much like plants and were often believed to be the connecting link between the plant and animal kingdoms, a view still held in some places. The coelenterates are simple animals, simple in the sense of their structural organization. They do not show the specialized diversity that obtains in the so-called higher animals, such as the insects, birds, fishes, and mammals. They lack the organs and tissues that characterize these animals.

A typical coelenterate, or polyp as it is commonly called, is simply a hollow tube open at one end, closed at the other. In cross section it is seen to be radially symmetrical, a condition in which all the parts are arranged about a common center like the spokes of a wheel. The internal cavity, in which digestion and circulation take place, is termed the gastrovascular space, and the open end is known as the mouth and is surrounded by a series of tentacles, each equipped with batteries of stinging cells or nematocysts. Hence the name *Coelenterata*, which is derived from two Greek words meaning "hollow" and "intestine." In the simplest cases the internal cavity is cylindrical in shape, but in the higher and larger forms it is much branched, forming a system of canals. In the typical polyp the parts that perform the different functions—digestion, circulation, respiration—cannot be distinguished from one another, and even in the higher forms little differentiation can be detected. What Shakespeare

22

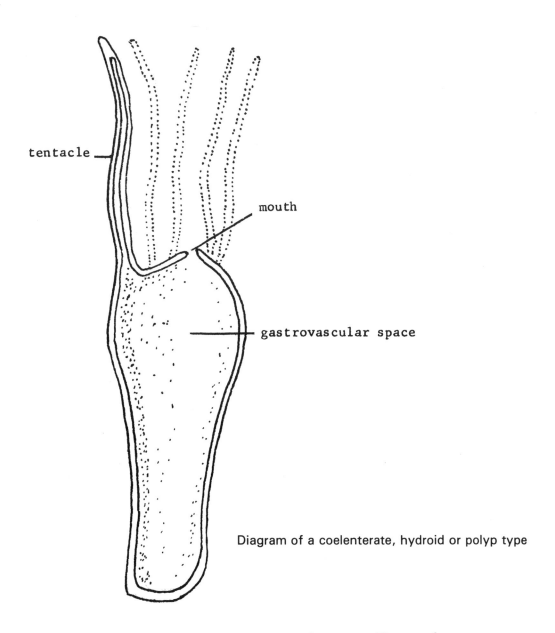

tentacle

mouth

gastrovascular space

Diagram of a coelenterate, hydroid or polyp type

said of old age can well be applied to the coelenterates: "Sans teeth, sans eyes, sans taste, sans everything."

The body wall of the coelenterates consists of two cellular layers, an outer, the ectoderm, and an inner, the endoderm. Among the cells that compose the ectoderm there are interstitial cells and often epithelial muscle fibers and nerve cells. Hence the ectoderm is both protective and sensory in function. Between the two cell layers is a membrane or tissue

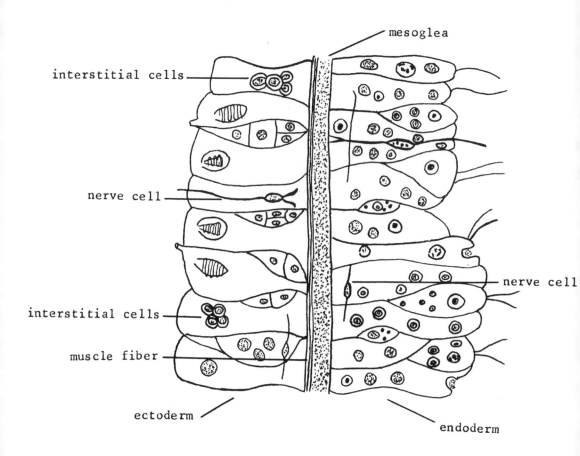

interstitial cells

nerve cell

interstitial cells

muscle fiber

ectoderm

mesoglea

nerve cell

endoderm

Longitudinal section of body wall of a coelenterate

known as the mesoglea. It is a supporting and skeletal layer and is thin, non-cellular, and jellylike in the coelenterates known as the hydro-medusans; in the other coelenterates cells migrate into it from the ecto-derm to form a third cellular layer.

Two distinctly different types of structure may be observed in the coel-enterates, although both have a common fundamental form. In the hydroid or polyp type, the body is cylindrical in form, one end being closed and usually attached to some stationary object, the other open and

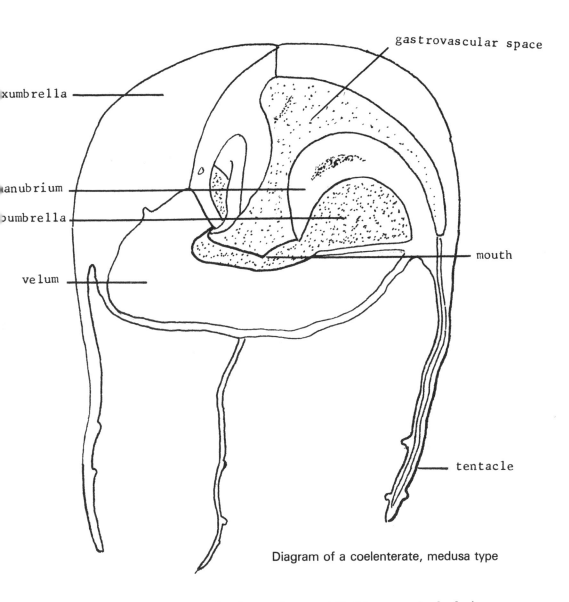

xumbrella

gastrovascular space

ianubrium

oumbrella

velum

mouth

tentacle

Diagram of a coelenterate, medusa type

surrounded with tentacles. In the medusa or jellyfish type, the body is more or less bell- or disc-shaped. The convex side, called the exumbrella, corresponds to the attached end of the hydroid polyp, while from the center of the concave side, called the subumbrella, there extends a more or less cylindrical, often branched projection, the manubrium, at the end of which is the mouth. The exumbrella, subumbrella, manubrium, and the edge of the bell may be provided with tentacles that can be long or short, flexible or rigid.

The coelenterates differ widely in form, size, and color. Whereas some occur in colonies and are stationary, others are free and independent; all, however, are aquatic. Their food consists of small swimming organisms or, in the case of the larger species, fishes of various size which are killed or paralyzed by the stinging cells. Food is taken in through the mouth and passed into the gastrovascular space where it is digested by enzymes. The products of digestion are then absorbed by the gastrodermal cells (the cells of the endoderm lining the gastrovascular cavity) and circulated throughout the body by the action of flagella or cilia, which are hairlike vibratory projections of certain cells. Respiration and excretion are performed by the general surface of the epidermis and gastrodermis.

Locomotion and movements are effected by the action of smooth muscle fibers, and the response to stimuli is brought about by nerve cells and fibers among the muscle fibers. Special sense organs are absent except in some species where they perform the function of sight or preserve equilibrium. Reproduction is by budding, the asexual method wherein new animals are formed by outgrowths of the body wall, or else by free-swimming larvae, the sexual method involving eggs and sperms. Typically there is an alternation of generations, one method being succeeded by the other. The hydroid, which is the asexual generation of certain coelenterates, may develop buds or offspring like itself, which may separate completely from the parent or remain attached to form a colony, or it may form cup-shaped buds that eventually separate from the parent as free-swimming jellyfish or medusae. These have an umbrella-

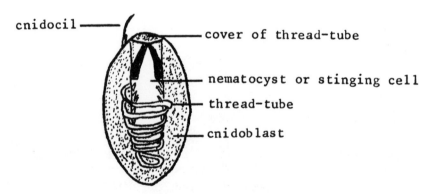

Nematocyst or stinging cell

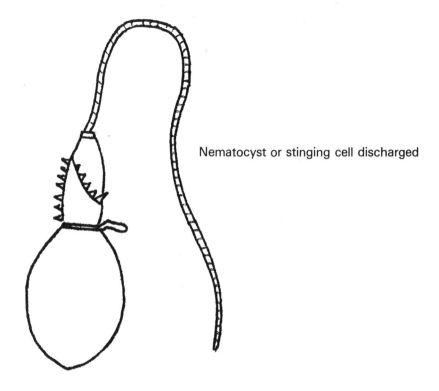

Nematocyst or stinging cell discharged

shaped body fringed with stinging tentacles, and a centrally located hanging tube which is suspended from beneath the umbrella like the clapper of a bell and which ends in the mouth. The medusae produce either eggs or sperms and the fertilized eggs settle on some stationary object to develop into hydroids that will repeat the process. Thus an asexual generation is followed by a sexual one and so on.

A characteristic feature of the coelenterates is the long vibratile tentacles equipped with stinging cells or nematocysts that render them effective tools in capturing prey. A nematocyst consists of a single special-ized cell in the ectoderm, called a cnidoblast, containing a cavity filled with a turgid liquid that surrounds a coiled hollow thread. A minute spine, the cnidocil, projects from the free surface of the cnidoblast into the water. When this spine is triggered by a suitable stimulus, presumably chemical, the cnidoblast contracts and the thread-tube is everted and shot out with considerable force. Barblike structures located within the hollow threads are brought to the exterior and penetrate an unwary animal. At the same time a poisonous fluid is ejected into it which kills or paralyzes it.

Zoologists have classified the coelenterates into three groups or classes: the Hydrozoa (hydra-like animals), the Scyphozoa (cup animals), and the Anthozoa (flower animals). The animals belonging to the first class typically have an alternation of generations in which there is a fully developed nonsexual hydroid stage and a sexual medusoid stage as described above. Most of them are polyp colonies but there are also individual polyp animals. The class includes the freshwater polyps (the hydras), the small jellyfishes, the hydroid zoophytes, and a few stony hydroids. In the second class, the polyp or hydroid stage is either absent or has become reduced to insignificance, and the free-swimming medusoid stage has become highly developed. The true or large jellyfishes belong to this class. In the third class, the medusoid stage has entirely disappeared. The animals belonging to this class are all marine polyps and are represented by such forms as the sea anemones, the corals, and the gorgoniums including the sea fans, sea pens, sea feathers, and the like.

The coelenterates number some 10,000 species, and though they are low on the evolutionary scale they cannot be dismissed as unimportant. They are an interesting group of animals of some economic importance, and may be used to illustrate many biological phenomena such as budding, regenerating, grafting, colony formation, metagenesis, polymorphism, and certain types of behavior. Anyone wishing to gain a better understanding of these rather exotic animals can do no better than to become acquainted with their freshwater representative, the hydra, an animal found in practically every pond, stream, and lake, and one which can easily be collected and kept in an aquarium, a bowl, even a bottle, with the minimum of care, to be observed and studied at leisure.

5. The Hydras

There are nine species of hydras in the United States. They occur in freshwater ponds, lakes, slow streams, sunlit pools, and even in roadside ditches where they may be seen with the naked eye hanging from plant stems or from the undersides of lily leaves. They are soft, transparent, cylindrical animals that can stretch themselves until they are half an inch or more long or contract until they are as small as pinheads.

When a hydra is extended it looks like a piece of string or thread frayed at one end. More realistically it resembles an elastic tube. The frayed ends are a circlet of tentacles which usually number six or seven, though in some species there may be as many as ten. In some hydras the tentacles are unusually extensible and can be stretched out from small blunt projections into very thin threads several times as long as the body. They act independently and function in capturing food and then conveying it to the mouth which they surround. The latter is a small circular pore in the center of a conical elevation (the hypostome) at one end of the body. Both the mouth and the hypostome can be dilated to a fairly large diameter when the animal is in the act of swallowing its prey.

The opposite end of the hydra is known as the foot or basal disk and is usually attached to some object. It secretes a sticky substance that enables the animal to anchor itself to submerged plant stems, twigs, or leaves, and even to the underside of the surface film of water. It also serves as a sort of locomotor organ: by clinging to an object with its sticky foot the hydra can glide along it and thus get from one place to another. It moves

29

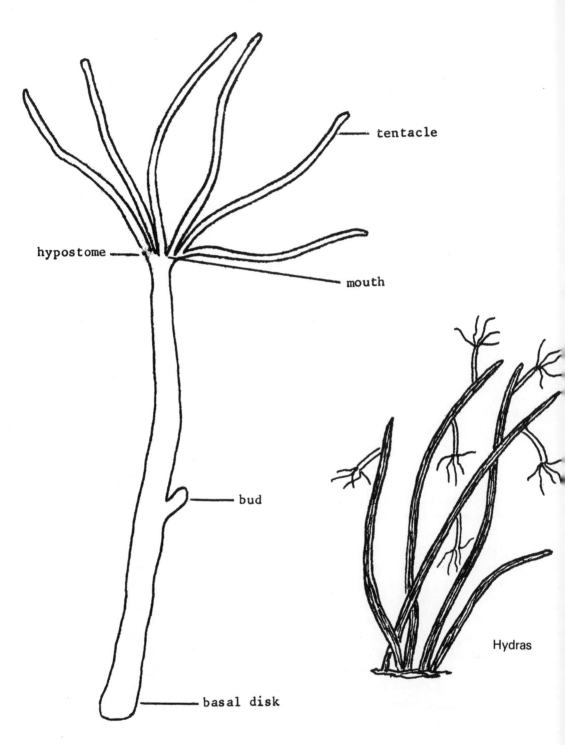

tentacle

hypostome

mouth

bud

basal disk

Hydra

Hydras

so slowly, however, that it is difficult to realize that it moves at all. In addition to the sticky substance, the foot also secretes a gas bubble enclosed by a film of mucus that lifts the hydra to the surface of the water, where it spreads out like a raft and hangs from the underside. In the foot is a pore which is completely closed while the hydra remains attached to some object but which is opened when the animal suddenly releases its hold. It is likely that the function of this pore is to enable the hydra to "blast" itself loose from its point of attachment. This is accomplished partly by a "peeling" action of the cells at the periphery of the foot and partly by the forceful expulsion of water from the gastrovascular cavity through the pore.

In common with other coelenterates, the body wall of the hydra consists of two cellular layers, the ectoderm, which is generally referred to as the epidermis, and the endoderm, which is commonly known as the gastrodermis. Between these two layers is a thin space containing a jelly-like material, the mesoglea, which serves as a supporting layer, as a basement membrane (the name given to a delicate membrane, usually composed of a single layer of cells, forming a substratum to the epithelial cells), and as a place for the attachment of the muscle fibers. Both the tentacles and body are hollow, the single central space being known as the gastrovascular cavity.

The hydras are carnivorous animals and feed principally on such small forms that live in the water as crustaceans, worms, clams, and insect larvae. Large hydras may capture and ingest young fish and tadpoles. In 1740 Abbé Abraham Trembley, the pioneer student of hydras, described their capture of baby fishes. Today hydras sometimes appear by the thousands in hatchery troughs and create a great deal of havoc among the small fry. Doubtless they act much the same way in their natural habitats.

Hydras are gluttonous feeders and will eat so much that their bodies swell out like meal-sacks, as one writer has put it, the food being visible through their transparent sides. Hydras, however, will not always make use of food available to them, as they will eat only when a certain length of time has passed since their last meal. In other words, their reaction to the food stimulus is determined by their physiological condition.

Normally hydras rest with the basal disk attached to some object and with the body and tentacles extended into the water. In such a position they are able to cover a fairly large amount of hunting territory. When prey has been captured it is conveyed to the mouth by the tentacle that has seized it, the other tentacles assisting in the operation and using their nematocysts to quiet the victim if it struggles and is likely to escape. Quite often the mouth opens before the prey has reached it, but once this occurs the edges of the mouth enclose it and force it into the gastrovascular cavity. Following ingestion certain gland cells in the gastrodermis discharge enzymes into the central cavity that at once begin to digest the food, the action of the digestive juices being made more effective by the repeated contractions and expansions of the hydra, the animal thus acting as a sort of stirring machine. The breakdown of the food is further promoted by currents created by the vibratory motion of flagella that extend into the cavity. Once the food has been digested, other cells in the gastrodermis, called nutritive cells, absorb the digested material, complete the process of digestion if necessary, and pass it on to the other cells

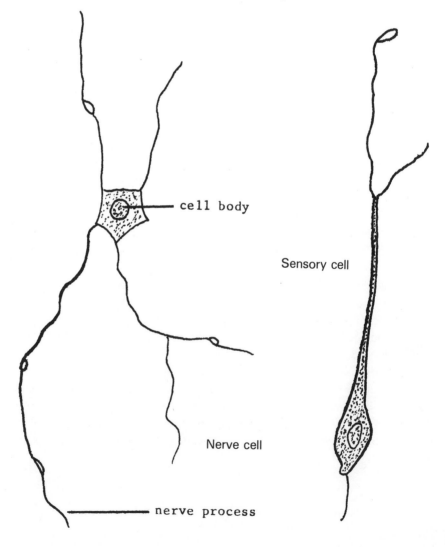

cell body

Sensory cell

Nerve cell

nerve process

of the body or store it for later use. All undigested materials and useless parts, such as the shells of clams, are ejected through the mouth by a sudden squirt, the debris being thrown some distance.

Hydras do not have any special structures or organs for respiration and excretion. Oxygen diffuses into the cells from the water in which the animals live, and carbon dioxide passes out in a like manner, and the wastes of metabolism are excreted through the general body surface. They do, however, have a simple nervous system, consisting of three general types of nerve cells (a nerve cell or neuron is composed of a cell body and protoplasmic extensions called processes), which are called conducting and motor cells, sensory cells, and sensory nerve cells. These cells form a network throughout the epidermis. At one time it was believed that their processes were continuous from one cell to the next, but it has been shown that although the endings of the fibers are in close proximity to each other they do not actually touch.

There are two places in the body of the hydra where the nerve fibers are concentrated: in the foot, and around the hypostome where they pass in a circular direction to form a loosely organized nerve ring. The conducting and motor nerve cells generally have several processes and can conduct impulses in any direction. The sensory cells are slender, thread-like, specialized nerve cells with sometimes a hairlike process or some other specialized structure at their tips. They occur both in the epidermis and in the gastrodermis, where they are more abundant in the region of the foot. Those in the epidermis are found mainly on the hypostome, on the inner part of the tentacles, and on the basal disk, places which are most sensitive to external stimuli.

Stimuli such as touch, light, and heat evoke a response in hydras to varying degrees. Touching the body or tentacles with a fine glass rod will cause the hydra to contract; merely touching one tentacle may result in the contraction of all the tentacles or of both the body and the tentacles. Agitating the surface of the water in an aquarium containing hydras will have the same effect. Once the stimulus has been removed, the animals will gradually expand and resume their original condition.

If a dish containing some water and a few hydras is so placed that it is not illuminated equally on all sides, the animals will migrate to the region where the light is brightest, though if the light is too strong they will seek a place where it is less intense. If the dish is placed in a dark spot the hydras become restless and move about aimlessly, but should they encounter white light their movements slow down and finally cease altogether. That such a reaction is of utmost importance to the hydras is evidenced by the fact that the animals that serve as food are attracted to well-lighted areas.

Hydras will move away from places of very high temperatures and will feed freely at low temperatures; hydras taken from ice-covered lakes have contained small insect larvae. Hydras kept in a dish will migrate from the bottom to the top if the supply of oxygen becomes exhausted. If subjected to a weak electric current, they will orient themselves with their anterior end toward the anode and the basal disk toward the cathode. Perhaps somewhat surprisingly, they do not react to water currents.

The reactions to stimuli are determined to a large degree by the physiological condition of the hydra, as, for instance, whether the animal will move upward to the surface and to light, or descend to the bottom, whether it will remain in a fixed position or move about and explore its surroundings, and how it reacts to chemicals and solid objects.

Hydras may move from one place to another by any of several methods. One method has already been mentioned, gliding along the object to which it is attached by means of its basal disk. A second method is what has been called a "measuring-worm" movement. In this method the hydra bends over and attaches its tentacles to the object to which it is already attached by its basal disk, then slides the disk up close to the tentacles, releases them, and assumes an upright position. The third method is by turning a series of somersaults. First it bends over and attaches its tentacles as in the second method. Then it releases the basal disk but instead of sliding it over to the tentacles it moves the disk completely over the tentacles and attaches it to the object again. The tentacles are then released and attached as before, and these movements are repeated again and again. In the fourth method, one which is seldom observed, the hydra moves in an upside-down position, using its tentacles as legs.

Locomotion and all other movements, such as those of the tentacles and the opening and closing of the mouth, are accomplished by muscles. The muscular system of the hydra consists primarily of two layers of contracting fibers applied to opposite surfaces of the supporting mesoglea. The outer layer is longitudinal and is formed by the contractile fibers of the epidermal cells, while the inner layer is circular and is formed by the contractile fibers of the gastrodermal cells. The circular muscle layer acts slowly but the longitudinal layer is capable of rapid response, which is to be expected in view of their location.

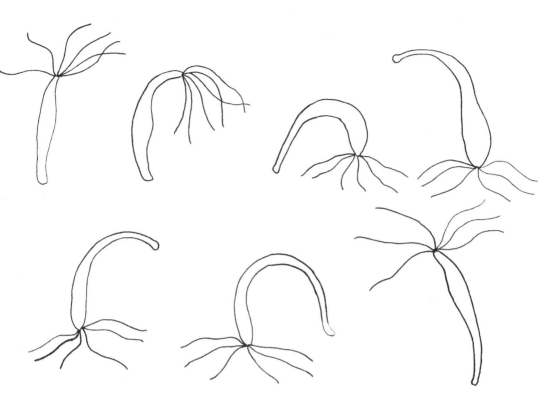

Movement in hydra by a series of somersaults

Hydras reproduce asexually by budding and sexually by the formation of germ cells (sperms and eggs). Both methods may occur at the same time in an individual hydra but usually they occur at different seasons. In budding the bud first appears as a slight bulge in the body wall. Once the bud is formed it pushes out rapidly as a projection and soon develops a circlet of blunt tentacles about its outer end. The cavities of both the tentacles and the body of the developing hydra are at all times connected with that of the parent. Even after the young hydra has acquired a mouth of its own and has begun feeding it will remain attached to its parent for some time, the food which it takes in remaining in its own gastrovascular cavity or being passed on to that of its parent. When the young hydra has become full grown it will become detached from its parent and take up a separate existence.

In some species of hydras, sperms and eggs may be produced in the same individual, in other species in separate individuals. The male germ cells are formed in small conical or rounded elevations on the body wall, called testes. There may be as many as twenty or thirty testes, and in most species definite nipples develop through which the sperms escape. The mature sperms swim about in the water in search of an egg; although several sperms may penetrate the egg membrane, only one enters the egg itself. The eggs are produced in the ovary, a larger swelling near the foot, which is less often present than the testes. Only one egg is formed in the ovary. Fertilization of the egg usually takes place soon after the egg is formed and while it is still attached to the parent's body. The early

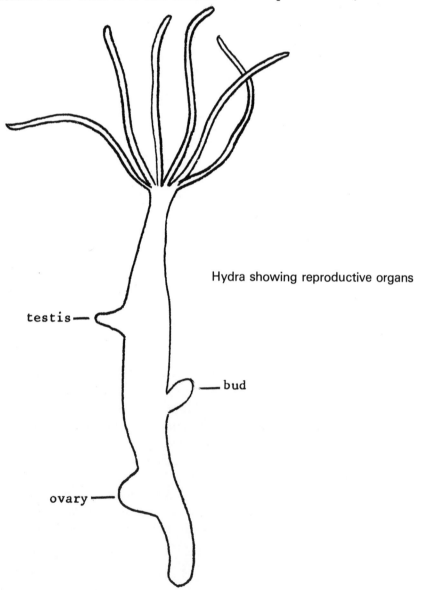

Hydra showing reproductive organs

testis

bud

ovary

development of the young hydra begins under a sort of parental protection but eventually the developing hydra or embryo becomes detached from the parent and falls to the bottom where further development takes place and a young hydra is formed complete with tentacles and a mouth. It is interesting to note that the sexual condition in some species may be induced by lowering the temperature, which accounts for the appearance in *Hydra oligactis* of sex organs in the autumn and during early winter.

Five of the nine species of hydras known to occur in the United States are dioecious, that is, the testes and ovaries develop on separate individuals. The other three are hermaphroditic with male and female organs on the same individual. In the dioecious species the testes cover the entire body region and are sometimes quite numerous; the ovaries usually appear first near the budding zone, which is about one-third the length of the body above the base, and from there spread up near the tentacles. In the hermaphroditic species the testes are near the bases of the tentacles and there are usually several of them. The ovaries are situated lower near the budding zone and there are usually only one or two at a time. Each testis produces hundreds of sperms but the ovaries only one egg each. As the egg matures it breaks out of its thin cellular covering and hangs out into the water ready to receive a sperm. No evidence is forthcoming that the eggs have a definite resting period or that they are latent over the winter, except insofar as low temperatures would retard the development of those that were produced in the fall.

Hydras produce buds abundantly at certain seasons and develop sex organs at others, but not all conform in producing either in the same season. In most species sex organs will develop out of season if the temperatures are favorable, and food is also an important factor, especially in the formation of buds. Generally hydras prefer cold to warmth. In water with a temperature of about 68° F. their reproductive capacity is apt to decline, whereas at a temperature of about 53° F. the reverse is true. One investigator was regularly able to induce the growth of testes and ovaries in species of *Pelmatohydra* within periods of two or three weeks by lowering temperatures to about 50° F. In warm pond waters their activity slows down and their populations decline, though other factors are also involved. In aquaria, and doubtless in their natural habitats also, hydras can stand a considerable range of temperatures if the changes occur gradually. They cannot stand sudden changes, however, something to bear in mind when they are kept in aquaria.

The stinging cells or nematocysts, already mentioned as being characteristic of the coelenterates, are present on all parts of the epidermis except on the basal disc, and are most numerous on the tentacles. They serve essentially in capturing the animals on which the hydras feed, but are doubtless of some value also as defensive weapons. In the hydras four distinct types of stinging cells occur, two of which are of use in capturing prey and are called penetrants and volvents, while the other two, known as streptoline glutinants and steroline glutinants, are used in locomotion.

The penetrants are large spherical nematocysts that are provided with three long spines and three spiral rows of small thorns on the base of the thread-tube, which when undischarged lies in transverse coils in the interior of the nematocysts. The function of the penetrants is to pierce the prey and to hold or kill or paralyze it by means of a poisonous secretion. The volvents are small pyriform or spherical nematocysts containing a thick unarmed thread-tube which makes a single loop inside the nemato-cyst and which is used to coil around the bristles or hairs on the prey and thus to hold it fast.

The streptoline glutinants are cylindrical or oval in form and have a thread-tube which is provided with a spiral row of small thorns along its length and which when discharged tends to coil. The steroline glutinants are oval or elliptical in form and discharge a straight unarmed thread-tube. Both glutinants are smaller than the penetrants and lack spines. They serve the hydras by attaching the tentacles to objects by means of a sticky substance, and thus permit the animals to move in a series of loops.

In 1740 Trembley discovered that hydras could restore lost or injured parts. He found that if the animals were cut into two, three, or four pieces, each piece would grow into an entire new animal. He also found that if a hydra were split longitudinally into two or four parts, each part would become a perfect polyp or hydra, that when the head or mouth end was split in two and the parts separated slightly a "two-headed" hydra would result, and that if a hydra were turned inside out the animal would readjust itself to the new conditions, the epidermal and gastro-dermal cells migrating past each other through the mesoglea until they regained their original positions.

By virtue of their ability to replace lost or injured parts, these animals came to be called hydras because of their resemblance to the mythical monster that lived in the lake or marsh of Lerna, in the Peloponnesus, and was finally slain by Hercules. The fabled hydra had nine heads and whenever Hercules cut one off, two grew in its place.

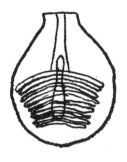

Penetrant

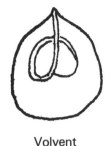

Volvent

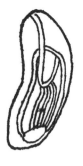

Streptoline glutinant

Steroline glutinant

The ability to regrow a lost part is known as regeneration and occurs not only in the hydra but also in other coelenterates and in animals of other phyla. Obviously the ability to regenerate a lost part is of benefit to any animal, since such a species is more likely to succeed in the struggle for existence under adverse conditions. Not only can the hydra restore a lost part, but parts of one hydra—even of a different species—may be grafted upon another. Many bizarre effects have been produced by grafting.

Hydras meet the dangers of low temperature by means of winter eggs which are formed and fertilized in the autumn. The eggs are encased in a protective shell, lie dormant over the winter, and resume their development in the spring. Hydras also pass the winter as adults, clinging to plants and litter at the bottoms of ponds and lakes; they have repeatedly been found beneath thick ice, and also at times abundantly in water near the freezing point.

A common species throughout the United States east of the Mississippi River is the Gray Hydra (*Hydra vulgaris, americana, grisea, stellata*). It is usually white in color but may be gray, orange, or brownish, is of moderate size with a slender body and about six tentacles that are always shorter than the body (from 1/4 to 3/5 as long), and has four kinds of stinging cells. This species usually has the male and female organs on different individuals but is occasionally hermaphroditic.

Also very common and widespread is the Brown Hydra (*Pelmatohydra oligactis*). It is brownish in color with a body that is slender at the attached end, three kinds of stinging cells, and about eight very long tentacles, three to four times as long as the body, and the sex organs occurring on separate individuals.

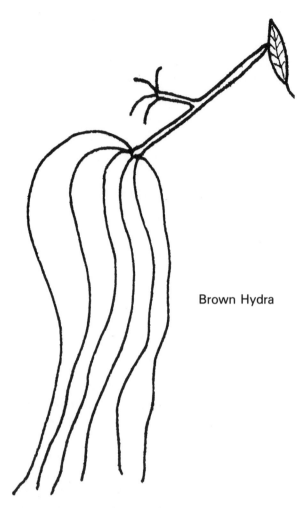

Brown Hydra

A third common species is the Green Hydra (*Chlorohydra viridissima*). It is grass green in color with about six short tentacles and is usually found on water plants. The green color is due to the presence of a unicellular alga, *Chlorella vulgaris*, in the gastrodermal cells. The plant makes use of some of the waste products of metabolism of the hydra, and the animal uses some of the oxygen that results from the process of photosynthesis in the plant, a give-and-take sort of relationship known as symbiosis or mutualism.

Unlike the three preceding species, *Hydra littoralis* lives in swift currents under stones, in waterfalls and spillways, or on wave-lapped shores. It has a stout body with tentacles 1 1/2 times as long as the body, and is usually pinkish or greenish orange in color. Adults can be found in all seasons of the year but are most abundant in autumn. They develop sex organs with falling temperatures in autumn and again with rising temperatures in spring.

When hydras are desired for study and observation they are best collected by gathering a few water plants like *Nitella* and *Elodea* and placing them in an aquarium or jar of pond water. If the animals are present they will soon be seen hanging out into the water. Tap water may be used but it should be allowed to stand for a few days. The hydras should be kept out of direct sunlight, and if new water has to be added from time to time it is best to add only a little at a time. Like other animals, hydras will have a better chance to live if they get used to the water gradually.

A few sprays of water plants will provide sufficient oxygen for them, and small crustaceans will be their best food. These can be obtained by dipping out some of the water close to the pond shore, or some species like Daphnia can be cultured. Hydras will even take a small worm or insect larva from a forceps if it is moved toward them very gently. In an aquarium one may observe their feeding habits, their various methods of getting from one place to another, and their general behavior.

6. The Hydromedusans

The hydras belong to the class Hydrozoa, as do the siphonophores, which have already been discussed, and the hydrocorallines, tubularians, campanularians, sertularians, plumularians, trachomedusans, and narcomedusans, which will be treated in the following pages. They are all generally known as hydromedusans with typically an alternation of generations of hydroid polyps and medusae. The hydroid stage is called the trophosome, the medusoid stage the gonosome.

The hydroid polyps are sessile and usually of colonial habit, but the individual polyps are small, generally being only a few millimeters in length. However, in some instances they may be several centimeters long, and in certain deep-sea forms as much as two meters or six feet. Quite frequently the colonies are plant-like in appearance. In a colony the individual polyps are called hydranths, the stalks on which they grow, the hydrocaulus, and the root-like projections by which the stalk is attached to the substratum, the hydrorhizae. All the polyps are in communication with one another as the gastrovascular space extends throughout the colony. In some species a cuticular layer, called the perisarc, is secreted by the ectoderm. It serves to give rigidity to the entire colony. The mouth of each polyp is at the free end, as in the hydra, and at the summit of an elevation, the hypostome. In many hydromedusans, the hydroid individuals are polymorphic, being specialized to perform different functions.

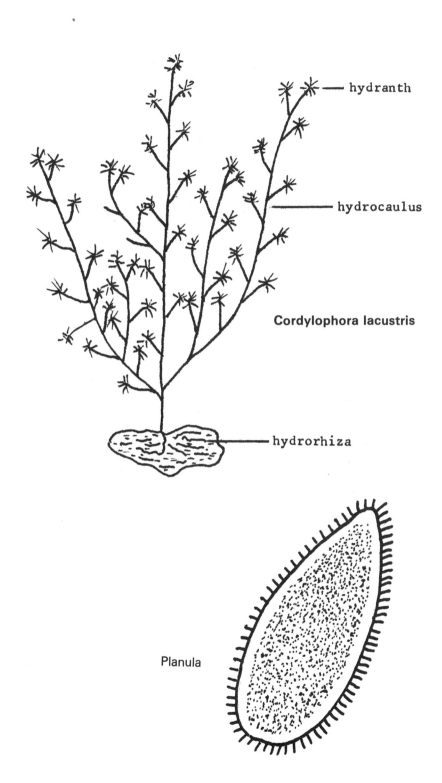

hydranth

hydrocaulus

Cordylophora lacustris

hydrorhiza

Planula

The hydroid polyp reproduces by budding off other individuals like itself or by forming a free-swimming medusa or a sessile medusoid individual or gonophore which remains attached to the parent, in which event it may have retained the general form of a medusa or be reduced to the form of a bud (sporosac) and have lost all likeness to the medusa form. The larva, called a planula, is free-swimming and ciliated, and following a period of active life becomes attached to some object and develops into a hydroid polyp.

Most hydromedusans are marine, though a few like the hydra, which is cosmopolitan in distribution, occur in fresh water. There are over 3000 species.

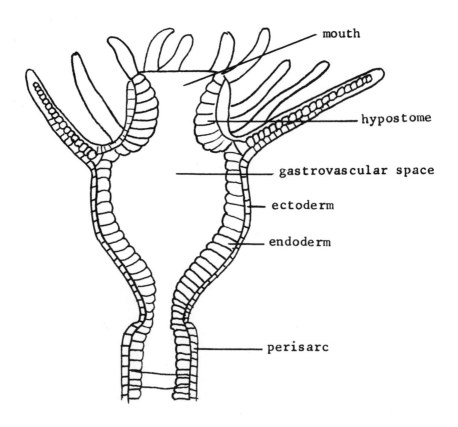

Diagram of a tubularian hydroid polyp

7. The Hydrocorallines

The hydrocorallines are hydromedusans whose polyps occur in colonies and which have a calcified cuticular outer covering (the perisarc) so thick that the colonies resemble corals. As a matter of fact these hydromedusans were once considered to be corals until their true nature was established by Louis Agassiz in 1859.

The colonies are composed of a network of tubes imbedded in a calcareous mass that is incrusted on a rock or some other object and that in the water extends upwards in the form of a more or less tree-like, coral-like body. The tubes have the cellular structure characteristic of the hydromedusans such as the hydra, the calcareous groundwork being secreted by the ectoderm. On the surface of the colony there are numerous pores which lead into cylindrical chambers. From the bottom of these chambers two kinds of polyps may project into the surrounding water. They are the nutritive polyps (gastrozooids) with the mouth end often provided with tentacles, and the defensive polyps (dactylozooids) that lack a mouth but that are furnished with batteries of nematocysts. The reproductive zooids are usually sessile medusoids or sporosacs, but in some species they are medusae which are produced in chambers that open to the outside through special pores.

The best known examples of the hydrocorallines are the millepores which form incrusting, branching, or foliaceous masses often of large size. They have a smooth surface with minute perforations for the zooids. The nutritive zooids each have four or five knobbed tentacles; the defensive zooids also have tentacles. The medusoid stage is represented by a free-swimming medusa having four or five rudimentary tentacles.

In the warm parts of the Pacific and Indian oceans the millepores are important reef-building corals. One species, the pepper coral, also known as the Elk-horn Coral, *Millepora alcicornis*, occurs on the coast of Florida and in the West Indies. In this hydrocoralline, each nutritive zooid or polyp is surrounded by five to six long and very contractile defensive polyps that have unusual stinging powers. Other members of the genus have similar stinging powers, and hence they are known as the fire corals, a name well deserved as they inflict a severe wound on an unwary diver.

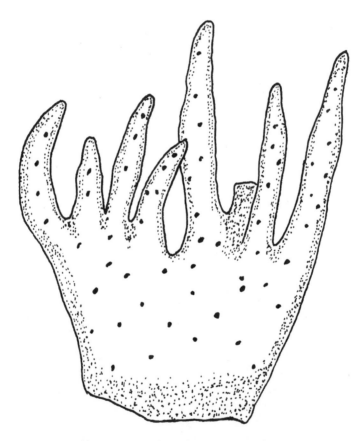

Pepper Coral, **Millepora alcicornis**

8. The Tubularians

The tubularians are colonial hydromedusans that for the most part have naked hydranths, that is, the hydranths are without a protective cup or hydrotheca. They produce either free-swimming medusae or sessile medusoid buds. The medusae, known as Anthomedusae, are usually more or less bell-shaped and typically bear the reproductive organs or gonads on the side of the manubrium. These form the eggs which settle down to a new hydroid stage. The margin of the bell is generally provided with a velum, a shelflike projection that partly closes the bell opening. On the bell margin at the base of the tentacles there occur eyespots of ectodermal origin.

If one should look in the tidepools along the Atlantic coast from Labrador to Long Island Sound, one would likely find the beautiful little hydroid *Clava leptostyla*. It occurs in velvet-like patches of reddish pink, and also spreads over the surface of rockweed (*Fucus*) in clustered patches and on wharf piles. The individual unbranched hydranths are club-shaped, about a quarter of an inch in height, and rise from a horizontal creeping network of stolons (hydrorhizae). From fifteen to thirty tentacles, each with a battery of stinging cells, are grouped in a scattered fashion about the enlarged head, which is surrounded by the mouth. The reproductive buds or sporosacs are formed in berrylike clusters just beneath the tentacles. The male sporosacs are pink, the female purple.

Unique in being one of the very few freshwater coelenterates, *Cordylophoro lacustris* occurs in the brackish water on the New England

47

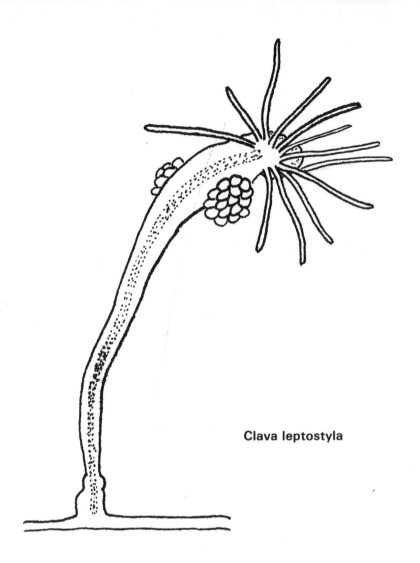

Clava leptostyla

coast and also in the inland lakes of the eastern and middle states. It is a profusely branching treelike colony and grows on stones, eelgrass, and wharf piles. It is one to two inches high. Each branch ends in a hydranth which has ten to twenty threadlike tentacles. The sporosacs, which are oval or ovate, are borne on the branches. This species is sometimes rather common.

A remarkable species that grows in colonies of polymorphic individuals is *Hydractinia echinata*, which is very common along the Atlantic coast and also in Europe. It usually grows on mollusk shells inhabited by hermit crabs, but may also be found on rocks, fucus, piles, etc. The polyps rise separately from an encrusted network of spiny stolons (hydrorhizae) and

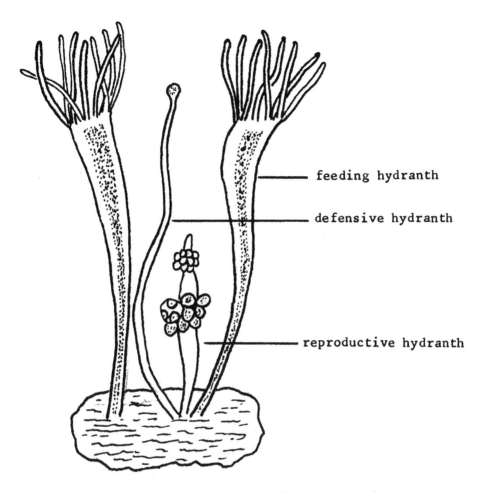

feeding hydranth

defensive hydranth

reproductive hydranth

Spiny Polymorphic Hydroid, **Hydractina echinata**

are of four kinds: nutritive or feeding zooids, reproductive or generative zooids, defensive zooids, and sensory zooids.

The nutritive zooids have simple, tube-shaped bodies that end in a mouth surrounded by a single whorl of threadlike tentacles. They obtain the food for the colony and pass the digested materials to the other zooids that lack a mouth. The reproductive zooids are generally shorter than the nutritive zooids and lack a mouth and tentacles though they are provided with nematocysts. They bear gonophores that produce sporosacs. The defensive zooids are intermediate in size and are more slender than the other zooids. They are usually more numerous toward the margin of the colony, and are usually without tentacles but have an abundance of

49

stinging cells at their apices. They are quite flexible and are generally coiling and uncoiling. The sensory zooids are somewhat like the defensive zooids except that they do not have the stinging cells but instead have sensory nerve cells.

Common from Maine to Florida is the bright pink hydroid colony *Pennaria tiarella*. It is found attached to rocks, seaweeds, eelgrass, and wharves below the low-tide mark. The plumes of the feathery colony are about four to six inches long, the main stems branching alternately, the branches at right angles to the stems and tapering, being shortest at the tops and the bottoms of the stems. The stems are covered with a hard, chitinous perisarc and are yellow to black in color. The feeding polyps (hydranths) are flask-shaped, with a whorl of ten to twelve threadlike tentacles at the base and also with a number of tentacles on the hypostome, each with a knob-shaped cluster of nematocysts. Along the sides of the hydranth, between the mouth and the base, medusa buds develop that eventually become free-swimming medusae.

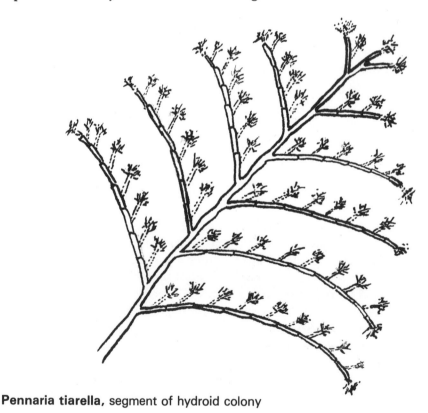

Pennaria tiarella, segment of hydroid colony

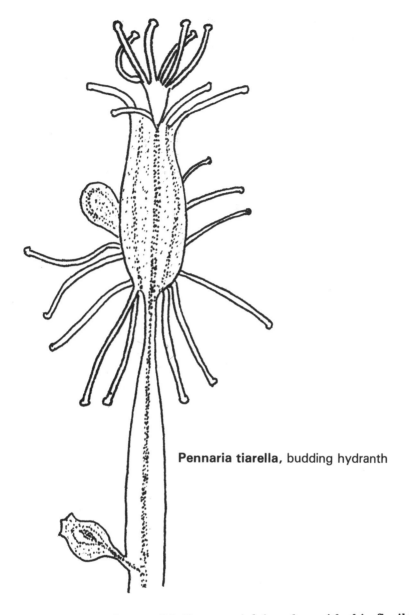

Pennaria tiarella, budding hydranth

The medusae are elongated bells, rose pink in color, with thin flexible walls, which in the female are sometimes distorted by the presence in the manubrium of four or five large eggs, and four small rudimentary tentacles at the base of each radial canal, the latter often spotted with deep rose pink through the rudimentary tentacles are pearly white. The medusae are free-swimming chiefly during the summer months, being more or less sessile during most of the year.

Common along the entire coast from New Brunswick to Florida, as well

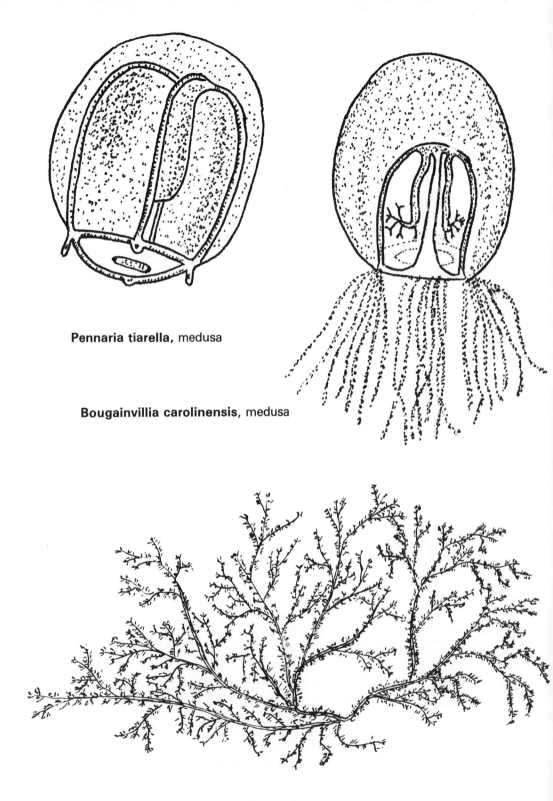

Pennaria tiarella, medusa

Bougainvillia carolinensis, medusa

Bougainvillia carolinensis, hydroid colony

as to the east coast of the Gulf of Mexico, the hydroid *Bougainvillia carolinensis* may be found growing on fucus, wharf piles, and the like. It grows in thick feathery clusters, with the stems forming loose networks that often reach a height of twelve inches. The hydranths each have a conspicuous hypostome and a single whorl of about twelve threadlike tentacles. The medusa has a globular or ovoid bell with a well-developed velum and trailing tentacles that are arranged in four clusters, each composed of about eight tentacles as long as the height of the bell. The four-sided manubrium is brick-red and flask-shaped, and there are four radial canals. Eight gonads surround the sides of the manubrium.

A related species, the Long-tentacled Hydroid, *Bougainvillia superciliaris*, occurs in the tide-pools of the Atlantic coast from southern New England to Greenland, and also in parts of Europe. The hydroid grows in clusters, about two inches high, and is attached to rocks or to mussel shells. The stem is red in color, very slender, and branches. Each hydranth has from fifteen to twenty slender tentacles in a single circlet. The medusa buds grow from the sides of the stem, encircled in a thin chitinous capsule. The medusae, which are liberated in great numbers in the spring, are nearly globular and less than one-half inch in diameter. The tentacles are long, are arranged in four clusters, and extend in every direction. The manubrium is four-sided, flask-shaped, yellow and short, and merges at the top into four radial canals. The mouth is concealed by four clusters of short treelike tentacles.

One of the largest of the tubularians is *Hybocodon prolifer* which is found from New England to Iceland and also in the waters about the British Isles and along the coast of Norway. It grows singly or in clusters of two or three, with no indication of a branching habit, in shaded tide-pools which are protected from the surf and in which the water is clear and pure. It is not a common species.

The hydroid is deep orange in color and quite handsome in appearance. It is about two inches high with a longitudinally striated perisarc which is annulated just below the hydranth. The mouth is located at the end of a narrow, cylindrical neck, which is capable of being extended, and there are two whorls of tentacles, each composed of about sixteen tentacles. Between the two whorls the gonophores are found in clusters that resemble a basket of fruit.

The swimming bell or medusa is hemispherical and asymmetrical, with a long, vaselike, tapering manubrium that ends in a four-lobed mouth. There is only one tentacle, the other three being extremely small and rudimentary, which accounts for the umbrella being asymmetrical in shape. From the base of the tentacle grow medusa buds which also

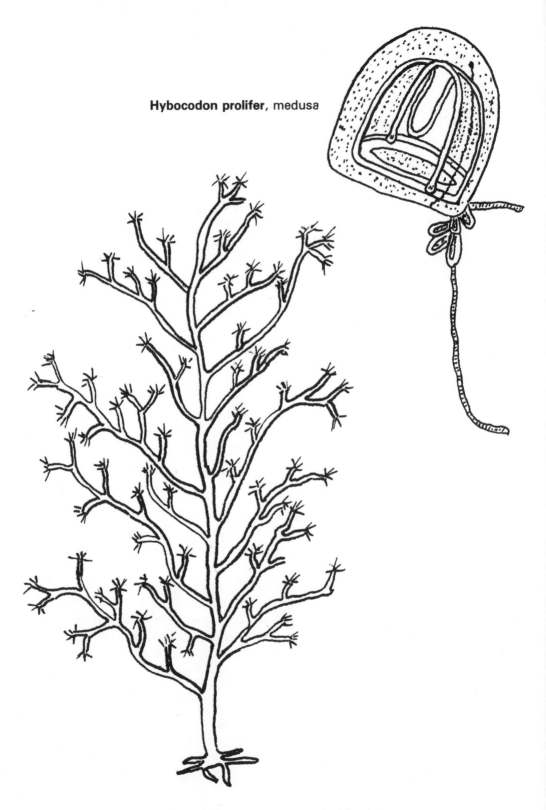

Hybocodon prolifer, medusa

Long-tentacled Hydroid, **Bougainvillia superciliaris,** hydroid colony

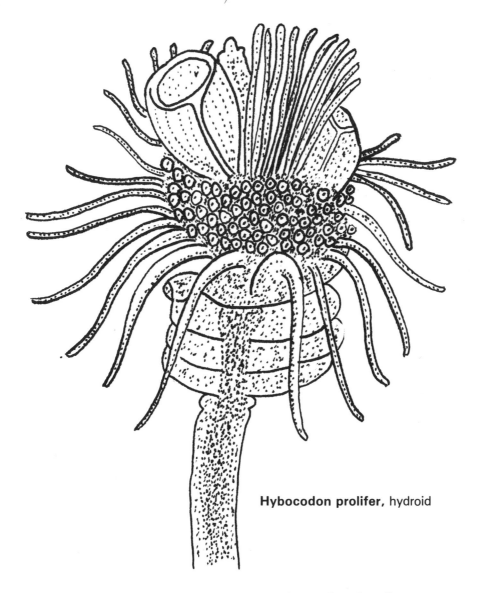

Hybocodon prolifer, hydroid

develop one tentacle each. When mature the medusa has five orange-colored bands.

From North Carolina to Greenland one may find the hydroid *Syncoryne mirabilis* growing one inch or less in height like tufts of moss on rocks between tide marks. The stems are elongate and slender, each being covered with a definite perisarc of transparent chitin and ending in a long bulbous hydranth which projects entirely beyond the end of the perisarc. The medusoid occurs in two varieties, one a sporosac with rudimentary tentacles and without eyespots or mouth, the other a free-

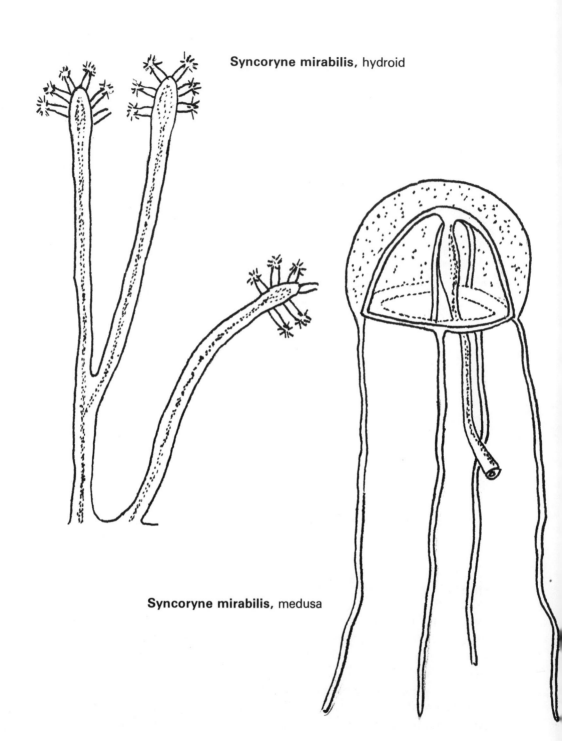

Syncoryne mirabilis, hydroid

Syncoryne mirabilis, medusa

swimming, beautiful, hemispherical and transparent bell up to one half an inch in diameter. It has four long threadlike tentacles and a very long, slender, greenish manubrium that extends far below the margin of the bell. There is a black eyespot within a greenish bulb with a brown center at the base of each tentacle and the gonads are borne on the manubrium which, as a result, becomes enlarged and fills the subumbrella cavity. The medusae develop in early spring and are very plentiful. They swim rapidly in all directions near the surface of the water. *Syncoryne mirabilis* may also be found along the Pacific coast from Alaska to California.

A loose treelike colony with many branches, arising from a branching, tangled hydrocaulus, is characteristic of the hydroid *Eudendrium ramosum*. It is abundant on rocks, piles, etc., from Labrador to South Carolina and it also occurs in Bermuda, Trinidad, California, and in Europe. There is a distinct perisarc, variously annulated, and the stems are more are less cemented together in bundles. The hydranths, which have a trumpet-shaped hypostome and a single whorl of some twenty-four threadlike tentacles, are usually located on the upper side of the series of the alternate but pinnately arranged branches. This species lacks a medusoid generation. The male sporosacs, which are reddish, bud in a whorl just beneath the tentacles, the female sporosacs, which are orange in color, usually above them.

One of the most beautiful of the tubularians is the Pink-hearted Hydroid, *Tubularia crocea*. This colonial hydroid, found from the Bay of Fundy southwards and from British Columbia to San Diego, grows in dense flowerlike clusters about one-half inch high with their bases much tangled. It is common on piles, wharves, and bridges in shallow water, and is bright pink in color. The hydranths have both a basal and a distal whorl of threadlike tentacles. There are no free-swimming medusae; the medusoids remain attached to the polyp, being suspended in a cluster like a bunch of grapes from long-stemmed stalks above the basal tentacles.

The beautiful and graceful hydroid of *Corymorpha pendula*, the Nodding Nosegay Hydroid, is solitary in habit and grows to a height of nearly half an inch. It is pendant and bright pink in color. It is common from Vineyard Sound to the Gulf of St. Lawrence and also occurs from North Carolina southwards. The hydranth has at the summit two rows of threadlike tentacles, one encircling the mouth, the other surrounding the base of the hydranth just below a ring of branching gonophores with medusae in various stages of development. The body of the polyp is slender at the top, gradually becoming club-shaped at the base, and ends

The Pink-hearted Hydroid, **Tubularia crocea**, a single hydranth

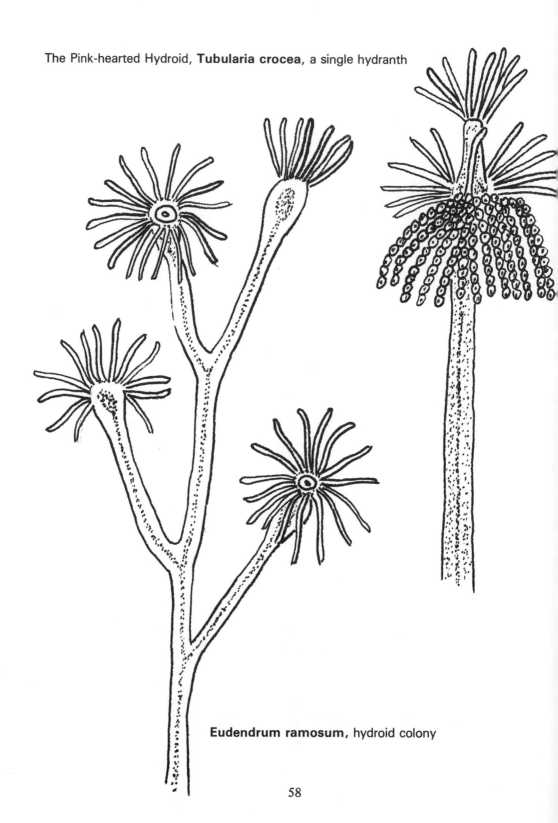

Eudendrum ramosum, hydroid colony

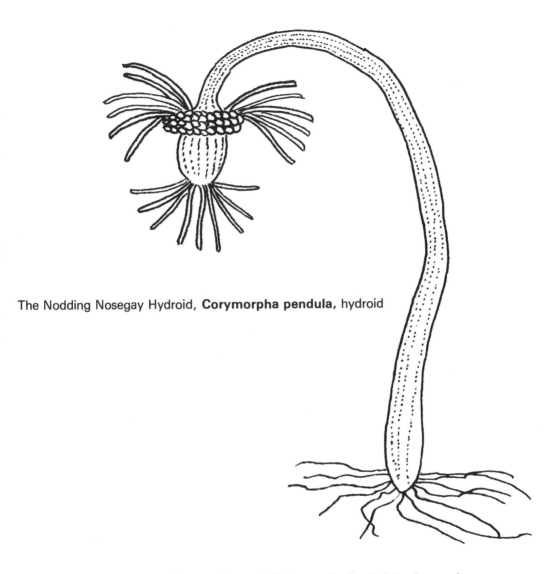

The Nodding Nosegay Hydroid, **Corymorpha pendula,** hydroid

in a branching, rootlike holdfast which is usually buried in the sand or mud.

The medusa is free-swimming and bell-shaped with a conical projection at the top. In the male this may be longer than the medusa itself. The medusa has four radial canals, a single trailing tentacle that is equipped with rings of stinging cells, and one to three rudimentary marginal tentacles. The manubrium extends to the velum.

9. The Campanularians

The campanularians are colonial hydromedusans with two kinds of polyps, the hydranths or nutritive polyps and the blastostyles or reproductive polyps. In the tubularians the perisarc ended at the base of the polyp but in the campanularians it continues over it, forming a protective cup called the hydrotheca in the hydranth and a cylindrical capsule called a gonangium or a gonotheca in the blastostyle. The open end of the hydrotheca may in some species be closed by plates or valves forming what is known as an operculum. Also the blastostyle in some species extends beyond the mouth of the gonangium and forms a large capsule, the acrocyst, in which the eggs develop. The hydranth has a single whorl of tentacles and can generally be extended beyond the hydrotheca or be retracted within it. The gonophores are produced within the blastostyle and may either be liberated as free-swimming medusae or remain in the gonangium where they produce planulae. The medusae, known as Leptomedusae, have marginal sense organs known as lithocysts instead of eyespots or ocelli. The gonads are borne beneath the radial canals on the subumbrella.

Typical representatives of the campanularians are the various species of *Obelia* (Laomedae). The hydroid colonies have a branched stem which may be simple or fascicled with flowerlike hydranths. The stem is ringed at the base of the branches and the hydranths and the hydrotheca often have an untoothed margin. The gonangia arise from the axils of the branches and have a small terminal aperture which is generally surrounded by a collar or neck. The medusae are more or less disc-shaped, have eight or more marginal tentacles, and have eight lithocysts

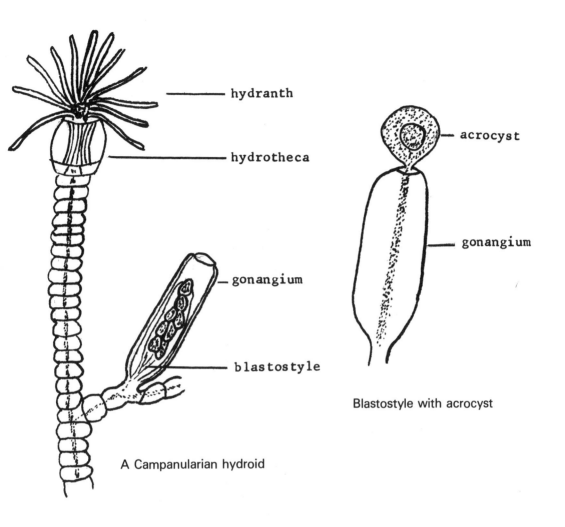

hydranth

hydrotheca

gonangium

blastostyle

A Campanularian hydroid

acrocyst

gonangium

Blastostyle with acrocyst

or sense organs that are situated around the margin of the umbrella between the bases of the tentacles. The medusae often swim with an everted bell.

A common species of *Obelia* along the Atlantic coast from South Carolina to Nova Scotia is *Obelia commissuralis.* It is a delicate, much-branched or treelike hydroid with a handsome appearance, and is found at low-water mark in tide-pools attached to stones and seaweeds, growing as much as eight inches long. Its branches are arranged spirally and spread nearly at right angles to the main stem. The gonangia are elongate with a distinct collar and arise on short pedicels from the axils of the branches. The medusae are free-swimming and have sixteen tentacles and four narrow radial canals, which give it a cross-like appearance.

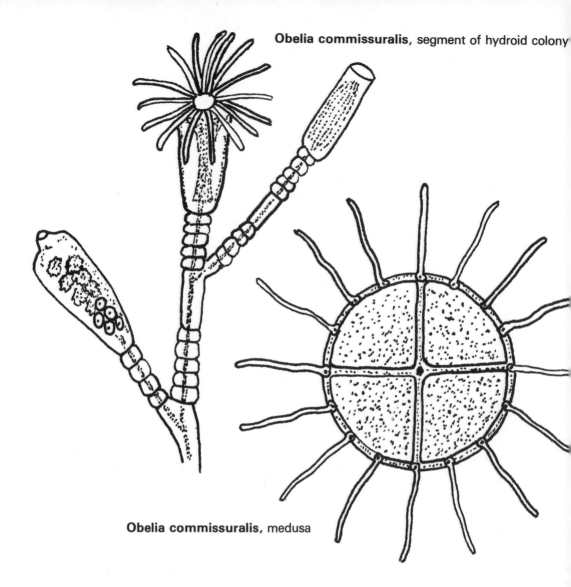

Obelia commissuralis, segment of hydroid colony

Obelia commissuralis, medusa

Also common from South Carolina northwards and along the Pacific coast from Alaska to California is *Obelia dichotoma*, the Double-branching Hydroid. This is a small hydroid, usually not more than an inch in height, which grows in erect colonies, either as a deep brown single stem without branches or, often, with zigzag branches. The pedicels of the hydranths branch off alternately at regular distances from each other. The hydrothecae are goblet-shaped with smooth margins and the gonangia are long and conical, rise from the axils of the stem, and have a collar around the terminal opening through which the medusae are liberated.

A cosmopolitan species quite common along the Atlantic coast and the

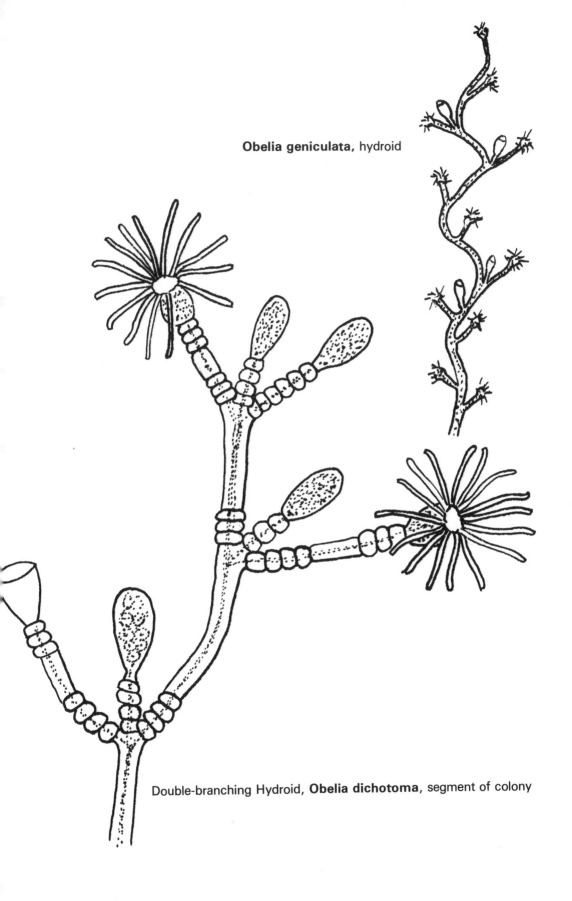

Obelia geniculata, hydroid

Double-branching Hydroid, **Obelia dichotoma,** segment of colony

coast of California, *Obelia geniculata* may be found on seaweed near the low-water mark as well as on wharves. This hydroid is also a low-growing species not more than an inch high, usually with a single zigzag stem bearing alternate hydranths on short ringed stalks. The hydrothecae are as broad as they are high and are quite conspicuous on the stem; the gonangia, ovate in shape, occur in the axils. The medusae are quite transparent, have sixteen to twenty-four tentacles, and their four gonads are located on the radial canals near the center of the bell. The medusae often swim with the bell everted, that is, turned inside out.

The many species of the genus *Campanularia* may be either branched or simple. These colonial hydroids have a cup-shaped or bell-shaped hydrotheca which is always at the end of a branch and which lacks an operculum. The hydranths have a single wreath of threadlike tentacles and the gonophores may produce either sporosacs or free-swimming medusae. Lithocysts are located on the margin of the umbrella and the gonads occur on the radial canals.

A typical species of the genus is *Campanularia verticillata*. This hydroid, which is found from Labrador to Long Island Sound, from Alaska to California, and in Europe, forms a plantlike growth with the hydranths appearing in successive whorls along the main stem. The hydrothecae are large and broad, the aperture having from twelve to fourteen blunt teeth, and are borne on ringed stalks which form a whorl around the stem. The gonangium is prolonged to form a neck and is sessile on the stem.

In tide-pools from Long Island Sound northwards, the hydroid *Campanularia poterium* may be found creeping over seaweeds. It also occurs along the Pacific coast and in Europe. *Poterium* is an unbranched colony, the hydranths at the end of ringed stalks which rise separately from a stolon or hydrorhiza; they are about a quarter of an inch high. The aperture of the hydrotheca, which is bell-shaped, is smooth, that is, without teeth. The hydranths have twenty-four tentacles and like the hydranths the gonangia also rise independently from the hydrorhiza. They are slender and ovate and are usually well filled with sporosacs.

A common species found at low-water mark from Vineyard Sound to Greenland, and from British Columbia to San Diego as well as in Europe, is *Campanularia volubilis*. This colony is also unbranched, with the hydranths at the end of long ringed stalks which rise independently from the stolon. However, unlike *Campanularia poterium*, the hydrotheca of *volubilis* has ten shallow-rounded or blunt teeth. The gonangia, which are flask-shaped, also rise independently from the hydrorhiza.

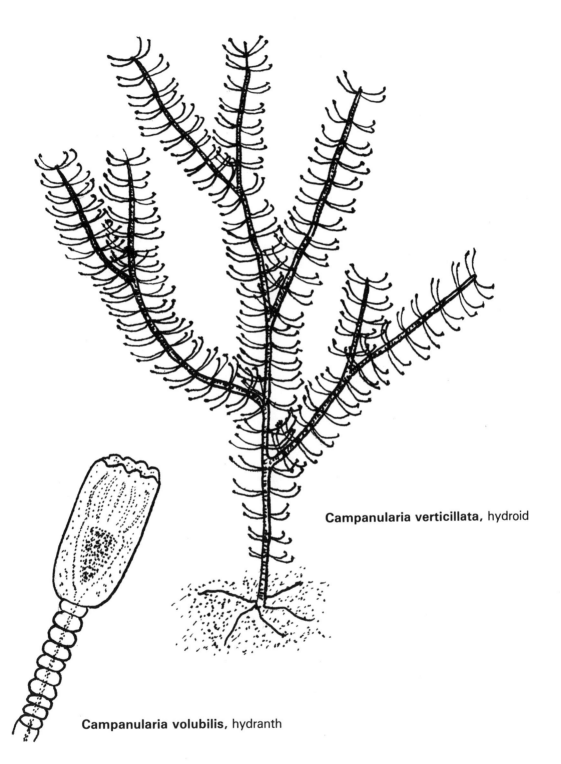

Campanularia verticillata, hydroid

Campanularia volubilis, hydranth

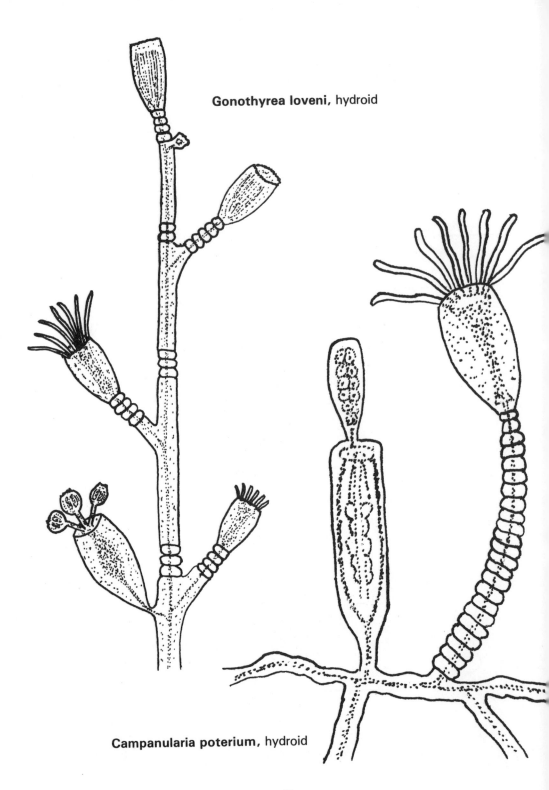

Gonothyrea loveni, hydroid

Campanularia poterium, hydroid

66

A colonial hydroid about half an inch or so high with a branched, wavy stem, the branches ringed, *Gonothyrea loveni* occurs on stones, shells, and the like in shallow water from Hudson Bay to Long Island Sound as well as in Europe. The hydrothecae are bell-shaped with ten to twelve teeth and the gonangia are elongated and sessile. From three to five sporosacs are formed in the gonangium and project out of the opening where they remain, there being no free-swimming medusae.

In many species of campanularians the hydroid form is unknown, only the medusae having been described. Such a species is *Eutima mira*, the remarkably beautiful medusa being quite common along the Atlantic coast. It is bell-shaped, not quite an inch in diameter and half as high, light blue in color, sometimes tinged with green, with four very long tentacles. The manubrium is very long and extends far beyond the bell, and the gonads are grouped along each of the radial canals for almost their entire length.

Another species in which the hydroid form has not been described is *Zygodactyla groenlandica*, the Many-tentacled Jellyfish, which has the distinction of being the largest of the Atlantic hydromedusans. The medusa is a beautiful jellyfish with a flattened disc, and measures from four to five inches in diameter. The subumbrella surface is shallow and flat or slightly concave, and the trumpet-shaped manubrium is broad above, narrowing to a cylindrical tube that again expands to a somewhat flaring mouth with frilled oral lobes extending beyond the velum. There are more than eighty radial canals, each with gonads, and from eighty to one hundred long slender tentacles around the margin of the umbrella. These, as well as the gonads, are of a delicate purplish pink color, the rest of the medusa being of a somewhat fainter tinge.

Another large species is *Tima formosa* whose bell is four inches in diameter and more than two and a half inches in height. The bell is hemispherical in shape with thirty-two tentacles around the margin. Eight of the tentacles are as long as the diameter of the bell, eight are intermediate in size, and sixteen, in the intervening spaces, are about an inch long. The manubrium is quite long, sometimes extending out of the bell, and surrounding the mouth are four frilled or ruffled projections. The gonads extend the length of the radial canals and the manubrium. This species has a small hydroid stage which develops from a free-swimming planula. The planula is pear-shaped and becomes elongated before it settles to the bottom of the sea where it forms a slender stem from which branch cup-shaped hydrotheca. *Tima formosa* occurs from

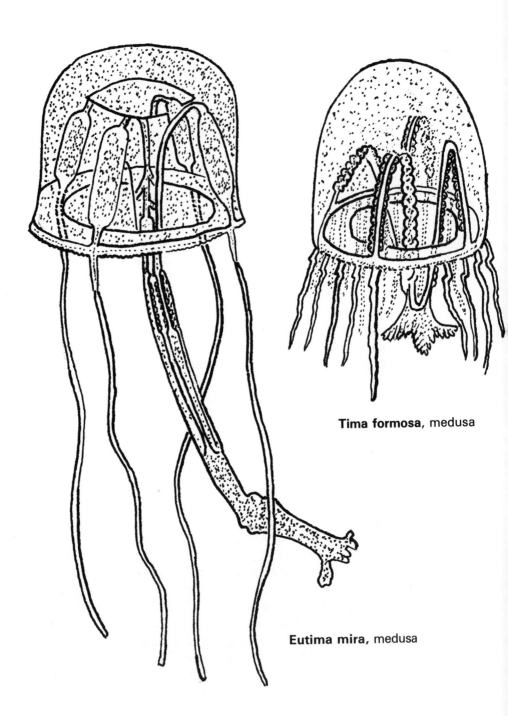

Tima formosa, medusa

Eutima mira, medusa

The Many-tentacled Jellyfish, **Zygodactyla groenlandica,** medusa

Cape Cod northward and is often common, especially in the spring and early summer.

A species with a hemispherical bell slightly flattened on the top with somewhat concave sides and about one half inch in diameter, *Tiaropsis diademata* occurs along the New England coast to the Arctic Ocean, as well as in Alaska. It has many tentacles that form a fringe around the umbrella margin, a narrow velum, a short manubrium with a frilled mouth opening, and eight sense organs. The gonads, which develop on the radial canals, are cream colored. *Tiaropsis* is often extremely abundant along the New England coast from March to May.

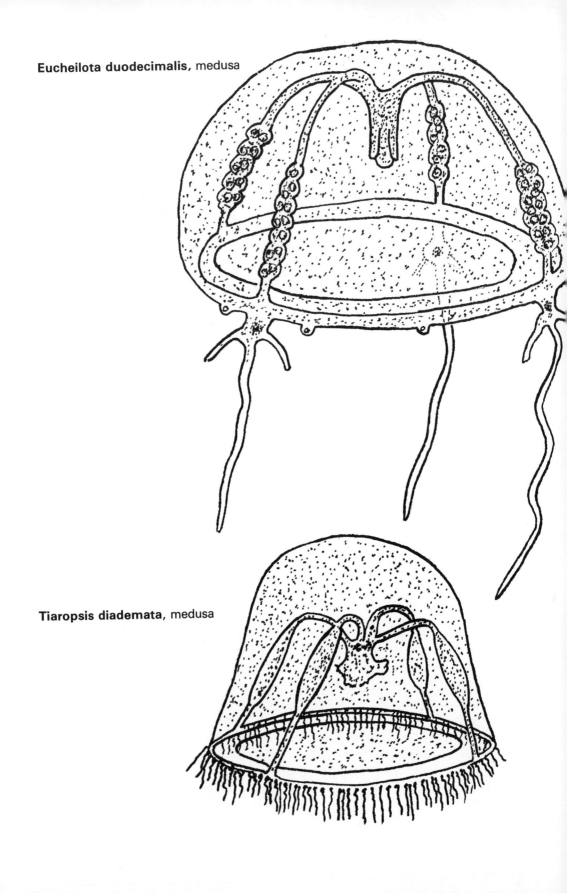

Eucheilota duodecimalis, medusa

Tiaropsis diademata, medusa

A very small but beautifully graceful medusa, *Eucheilota duodecimalis* is found from Cape Cod to Florida and is often very common. The bell is slightly more than hemispherical, about one-tenth of an inch in diameter, with four tentacles, each with two short, slender, and conical cirri at its base. The manubrium is quadrangular in section and quite short and the velum is well developed. The gonads are located on the outer portion of the radial canals, the female gonads being extremely large and conspicuous.

Strikingly beautiful in outline is the pear-shaped medusa of *Melicertum campanula* which occurs from Cape Cod northward to Greenland and also along the coast of Europe. It is light ochre in color, the bell about an inch in height, and the margin of the umbrella with about seventy or eighty long, slender tentacles. The manubrium is short with fluted sides and eight flaring lips. There are eight radial canals with the gonads running their entire length. The eggs develop into free-swimming, ciliated, pear-shaped planulae which become attached to the sea bottom by the large end. Here the narrower free end lengthens into a tubular projection which becomes the stem of an elongate minute hydroid. The hydrothecae are funnel-shaped and the hydranths have about twelve short and stumpy tentacles.

In the various species of *Halecium* the hydrothecae are more or less rudimentary, being funnel-shaped tubes and so shallow that the hydranths are exposed even when contracted. The margin is smooth and often ornamented with a circle of dots. The reproductive polyps give rise to planulae and never to free-swimming medusae. *Halecium halecinum* is a bushy colony, from four to eight inches high, of several main stems with the branches extending from them feather-fashion. The hydrothecae are set alternately on the branches. The gonangia occur in rows on the branches, the male gonangium slender and club-shaped, the female somewhat irregular in shape with a broad distal end and a terminal opening. This species is found in shallow water from New Jersey to Labrador, from Alaska to Puget Sound, and also along the coast of Europe.

A delicate colony with few branches and only about three-fifths of an inch in height, *Halecium tenellum* is found along the North American coast from New Brunswick to Florida and from the Aleutian Islands to San Diego in depths varying from eight to forty or fifty fathoms. The stem is irregularly branched and is sometimes wavy or ringed. The hydrothecae are trumpet-shaped and occur alternately on the branches; the

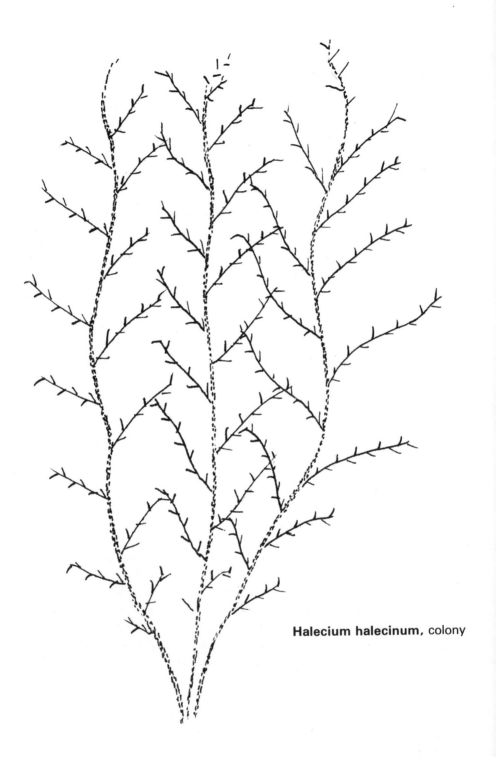

Halecium halecinum, colony

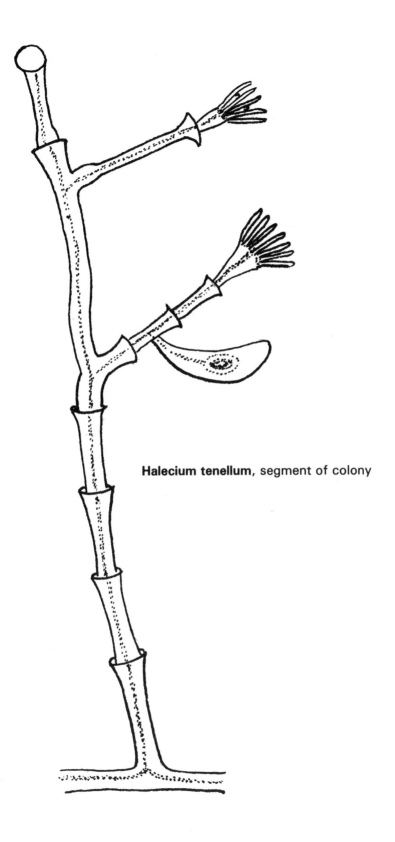

Halecium tenellum, segment of colony

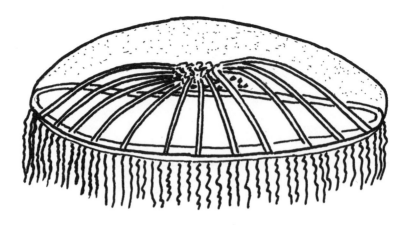

Aequorea tenuis, medusa

gonangia, which arise from the axils of the branches of the main stem, are bladderlike and somewhat oval.

The species *Aequorea tenuis* occurs irregularly in Vineyard and Long Island Sounds and is popularly known as the Flat Jellyfish. The hydroid form is minute and generally unknown. The medusa is disc-shaped or hemispherical, with a diameter of one and a half to four inches. It has a short, wide manubrium, from twenty to forty radial canals with an equal number of gonads, and many long and slender tentacles each having a spur above the base.

10. The Sertularians

The sertularians are colonial hydroids, usually branching, with sessile hydrothecae, that is, the hydrothecae are set directly against the stem instead of being raised upon a stalk. Most of the hydrothecae have opercula and most bud from both sides of the stems and branches in two longitudinal rows that are either opposite to each other or alternate. In some instances, however, the hydrothecae bud from only one side of the stem, their opercula turned alternately to the right and left. The gonangia are much larger than the hydrothecae, each containing a blastostyle that produces planulae, there being no free medusae. There are only a few gonangia in a colony and they occur only at certain times of the year.

The sertularians are found everywhere along the Atlantic coast, where they may be seen forming zigzag patterns over the fronds of seaweed or hanging in fringes from them, as well as upon rocks and shells. They are often mosslike or fernlike, at times forming beautiful and delicate plumes that float out in the water, and have often been gathered by amateur collectors who have mistaken them for seaweeds.

One of the most abundant of the sertularians, indeed, one of the most abundant of all the hydroids on the northeast coast, is *Sertularia pumila*, the Wreathed Hydroid. It is common on fucus and other seaweeds between tide-lines and is a simple or more or less branched colony, the erect stems often being two inches long. The colony is attached by a creeping root-stalk, the stem being divided into short internodes, each bearing a pair of hydrothecae, the members of the pair being directly

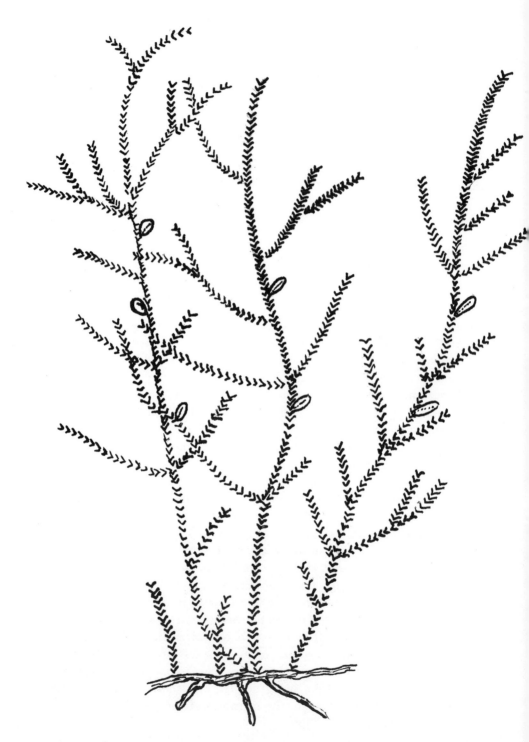

The Wreathed Hydroid, **Sertularia pumila**, colony

opposite each other. The gonangia are oval or urn-shaped, sessile, and have a wide opening with a shallow rim at the summit. The male gonangium is rather more slender than the female.

Found all along the entire Atlantic coast from Georges Bank to Florida, the West Indies, and the Leeward Islands as well as along the coast of Europe, *Sertularella gayi* is a colony with paired or alternate rather stiff branches, the colony sometimes six inches in length, and with the hydrothecae set alternately on the stem and not opposite as in the preceding species. The hydrothecae are wrinkled or partially ringed, with

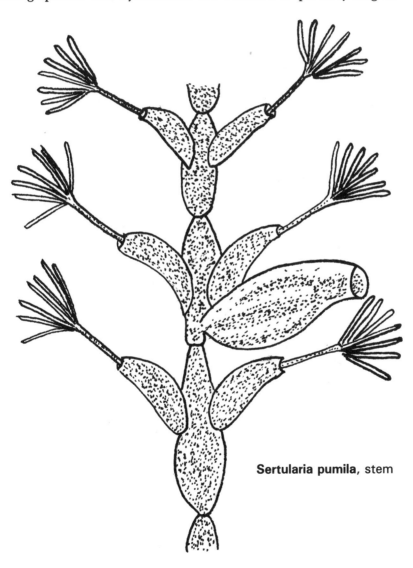

Sertularia pumila, stem

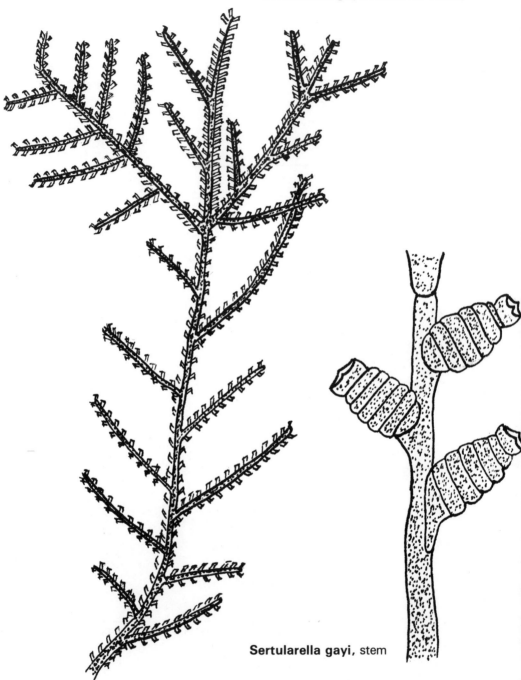

Sertularella gayi, branch of colony

Sertularella gayi, stem

four teeth on the margin. The gonangia, on the upper sides of the branches, are long and slender and taper towards both ends.

Growing from the stems of various seaweeds in all directions, *Sertularella rugosa* is a small colony not quite an inch high that ranges from New England to Labrador, also from Alaska to San Francisco Bay and along the coast of Europe. The colony may be either unbranched or slightly branched, the stem more or less ringed and rough. The hydrothecae are alternate, with horizontal ridges or rings, and four marginal teeth. The operculum is prominent and is composed of four triangular sections. The gonangia are large and conspicuous, are also ringed, and have a four-toothed aperture.

A common species along the New England coast north to Hudson Bay, also from Alaska to San Diego and along the coast of Europe, *Sertularella tricuspidata* is a delicate, loosely branching colony found growing from the stems of various seaweeds. It is not quite five inches high, slender,

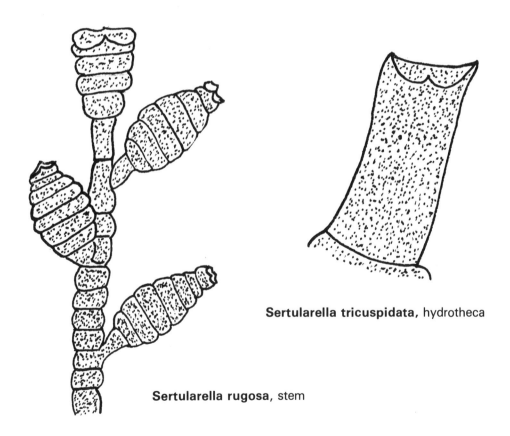

Sertularella tricuspidata, hydrotheca

Sertularella rugosa, stem

79

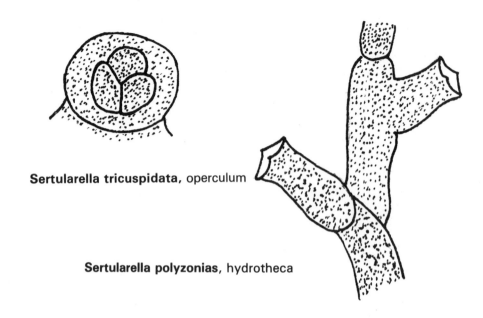

Sertularella tricuspidata, operculum

Sertularella polyzonias, hydrotheca

with alternate branches. The hydrothecae are set alternately on the stem, somewhat separated from each other, have three marginal teeth and an operculum of three valves. The gonangia are oval and conspicuously ornamented with horizontal, thin, shelflike ridges around the urn-shaped gonotheca.

Sertularella polyzonias is a cosmopolitan species and quite common, occurring along both the Atlantic and Pacific coasts. It is an irregularly branching colony not quite five inches high with the hydrothecae being relatively large and urn-shaped, extending obliquely from the stem. They have four teeth and an operculum of four parts. The gonangia, also with four teeth, are deeply ringed.

A large, bushy and conspicuous colony, often more than a foot high, the species *Thuiaria argentea* is common from the Arctic Ocean along the Atlantic coast south to Cape Hatteras, and from Alaska to San Francisco Bay from low-water mark to one hundred fathoms, usually in rather deep water. It has a profusion of silvery branches that arise from all sides of a dark stem, each branchlet dividing into two parts. The hydrothecae alternate with each other, more than a pair to an internode, for the most part embedded in the stem, the margin with two teeth, one of which is usually longer than the other. The gonangia, which have an elongated triangular form tapering towards the base, with a circular opening and usually two spines, spring from the base of the hydrothecae. *Thuiaria*

80

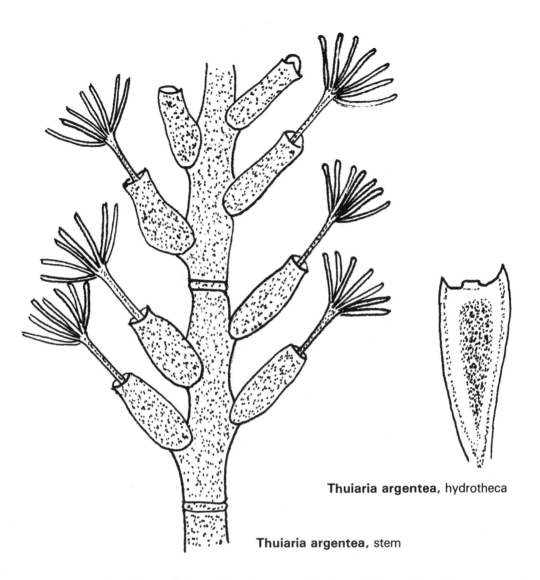

Thuiaria argentea, hydrotheca

Thuiaria argentea, stem

argentea is a beautiful species, its name hinting of its rather silvery, shining appearance.

Sometimes almost a foot in height and found in shallow water from the northerly coast of New England to the Gulf of St. Lawrence, as well as from the Bering Sea to the San Juan Islands and along the coast of Europe, *Thuiaria thuja* is a rigid colony, the main stem stiff and zigzag in contour, the branches forming a symmetrical spiral of palmate growth. The result is a stiff, dense tuft which has given to the colony the popular name of Bottlebrush. The hydrothecae are tubular and alternate, lack teeth, and have but one flap to the operculum. The gonangia are smooth

81

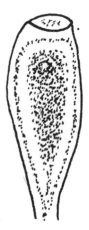

Thuiaria thuja, hydrotheca

Thuiaria thuja, stem

and pear-shaped with a collared aperture and form rows at the base of the branches.

From New Jersey to the Arctic Ocean, *Thuiaria cupressina* occurs from low-water mark to 150 fathoms. It is a slender, elongated colony, often eight inches high, with a somewhat wavy stem from which alternately extend plumelike tufts of branches. The hydrothecae are in pairs and alternate, the margin of the aperture with two rather inconspicuous teeth, the operculum with two flaps. The gonangia are elongated with a

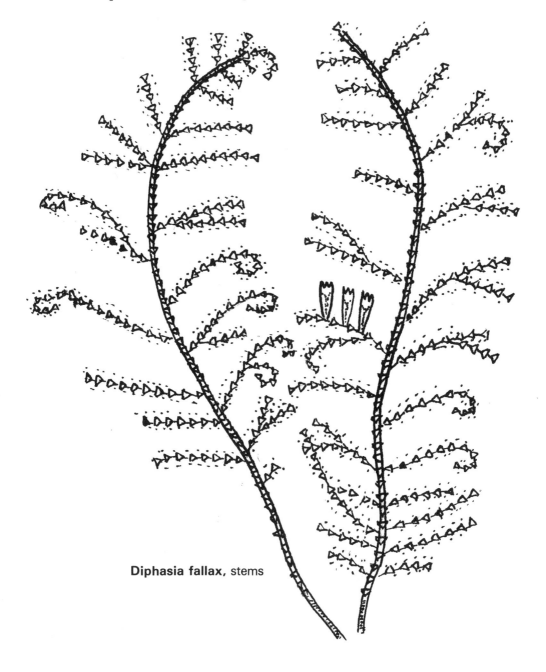

Diphasia fallax, stems

conspicuous spine at each side of the aperture and are therefore quite characteristic. This species is sometimes popularly called the sea cypress.

In the species *Diphasia fallax* the stem is erect and branches to form graceful clusters that end in the manner of tendrils. The hydrothecae are short and stout, occur in pairs opposite each other, and stand out from the stem. They have a one-valved operculum. The gonangia are large and conspicuous and are dimorphic. The male gonangium is spindle-shaped with a central tubular orifice and four spines or projecting lobes; the female gonangium is larger, oval, and is deeply cleft into four segments. The colony is sometimes as long as four inches and occurs abundantly from Massachusetts Bay to the Bay of Fundy, as well as along the coast of Europe.

A common and related species found from Labrador to Vineyard Sound and also along the coast of Europe, *Diphasia rosacea* is a delicate colony with a few alternating branches and is about four inches long. The hydranths are rather slender. The male gonangium is pear-shaped with eight longitudinal ridges that end in teeth which surround the opening; the female gonangium is larger with two long, low lobes and six shorter ones.

In the species *Hydrallmania falcata* popularly called "coral moss," the hydrothecae are seated in a single row on only one side of the branch but bend alternately to the right and to the left. The colony, which often grows to a foot in length, has a long, undulating, slender stem from which

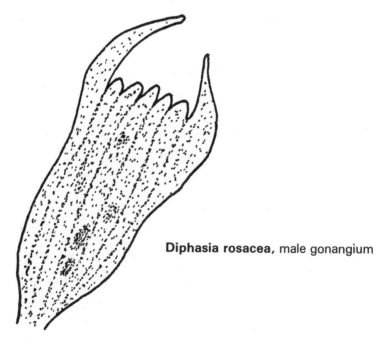

Diphasia rosacea, male gonangium

branches extend more or less alternately; these have secondary branches which are very regular and featherlike. The gonangia are egg-shaped, smooth, and without spines. The colony grows on stones, shells, etc., and is quite common from Long Island Sound north to the Arctic Ocean and along the coast of Europe.

Hydrallmania falcata, stem

11. The Plumularians

The plumularians are colonial hydroids that have a characteristically plumelike or featherlike effect, since the short lateral branches are arranged on each side of a long central stem and since the sessile hydranths are set in a row on only one side of the branches, which are called hydrocladia. Small defensive polyps called nematophores occur between the hydranths and on the main stem, each consisting of a hydrotheca and an elongated body armed with nematocysts. The gonangia, which are large and often bladderlike, produce planulae and never medusae. There are over 300 species of plumularians, which constitute a quarter of all the known hydroids. Most of them are tropical but a number may be found along the Atlantic and Pacific coasts and in the West Indies.

Occurring along the New England coast from Martha's Vineyard to the Bay of Fundy in depths of six to sixty fathoms, and also along the coast of Europe, the colonial hydroid *Antennularia antennina* is a dense cluster of upright stems, often eight inches high, with few branches (hydrocladia), the branches in whorls at the internodes and bearing the hydranths and nematophores. The hydrothecae are small and cup-shaped, the gonangia ovate and rather large. Another species of the same genus, *Antennularia americana*, found along the New England coast in depths of fifty to 120 fathoms, is about eight to ten inches in height and sparsely branched if at all. It is much like the preceding species except that there are more internodes.

Of a striking appearance, *Monostaechas quadridens* consists of a thin,

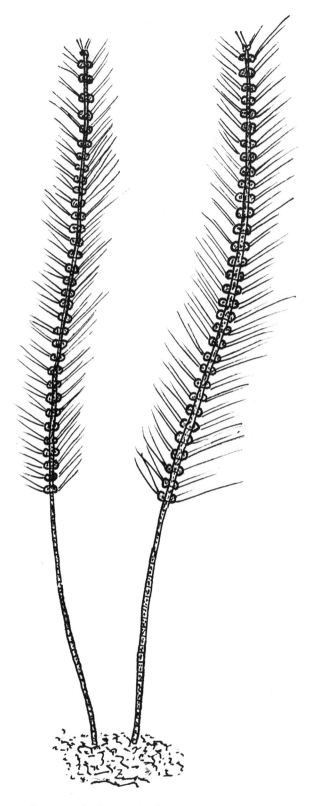

Antennularia antennina, stems

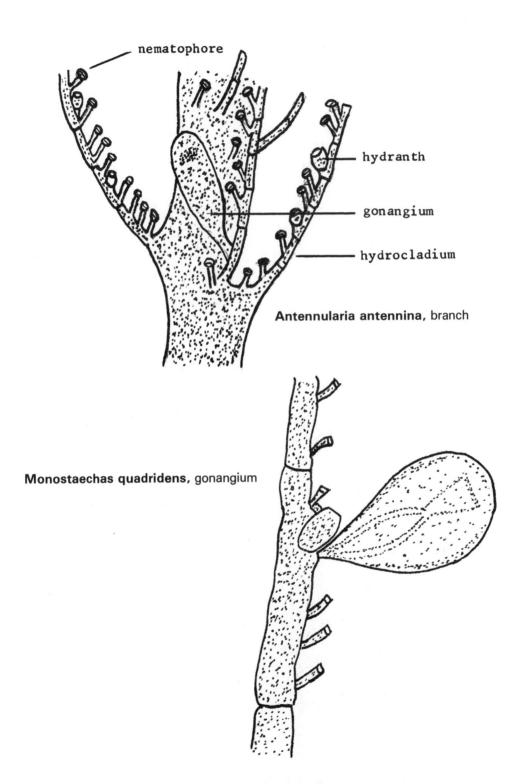

nematophore

hydranth

gonangium

hydrocladium

Antennularia antennina, branch

Monostaechas quadridens, gonangium

elongated stem which divides into two branches, the branches in turn dividing into a series of long, slender hydrocladia. The entire colony attains a height of about six inches. Each of the hydrocladia consists of a series of short internodes, with a cup-shaped hydrotheca growing out diagonally on nearly every other internode. All the hydrocladia spring from the upper side of the branches and rise vertically and parallel to each other. The gonangia are oval in shape and rise from a stemlike projection just beneath a hydrotheca, the nematophores being borne on very slender, elongated stems that spring from the bases of the hydrothecae. The species occurs from Martha's Vineyard southwards to Florida.

The hydroid *Schizotricha tenella* is a delicate colony about two inches high found from the Bay of Fundy southwards to North Carolina. The species has a slender, zigzag stem which bears branching hydrocladia. The hydrothecae are small and occur on every other internode, two or three nematophores occurring between them. The gonangia are shaped like cornucopias and grow from near the base of the hydrotheca. The colony often grows on piles and the like in shallow water.

Along the New England coast as well as along the coast of Europe there occurs a related species, *Schizotricha gracillima*. It is about the same height as the preceding and has a fascicled zigzag stem from which rise alternate double branches. The hydrothecae are cup-shaped and occur on about every other internode, the nematophores are large and have two chambers, and the gonangia rise in pairs on the lower part of the stem and are cylindrical in shape.

A common species, *Cladocarpus flexilis* occurs in moderately deep water along the Atlantic coast. The colony may be as much as nine inches high and has a long central stem with hydrocladia on either side producing a featherlike structure. The hydrothecae are long and cylindrical, lie close to the hydrocladia, the aperture of each with a large median tooth and several small tooth-shaped projections on either side. The gonangia are numerous and are borne on the stem at the base of the hydrocladia. They are club-shaped in appearance and their protecting branchlets are branched like deer's horns. These branchlets are armed with nematophores.

There are about twenty-five American species of the genus *Plumularia*. The hydrocladia are unbranched and pinnately arranged, with each having more than one hydrotheca, the latter with an entire margin. The colonial hydroid *Plumularia setacea* occurs off Key West, and from Vancouver Island to San Diego, from low tide to twenty-five fathoms. The

89

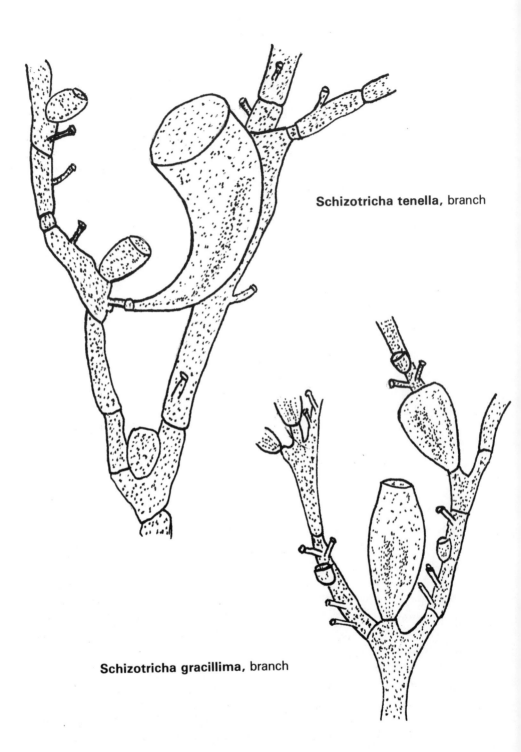

Schizotricha tenella, branch

Schizotricha gracillima, branch

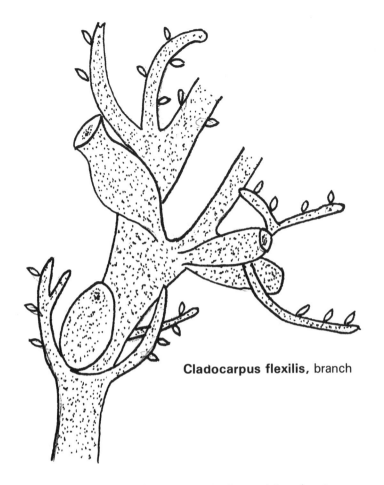

Cladocarpus flexilis, branch

colony reaches a height of about two inches, with a simple stem and alternate hydrocladia in the same plane. The gonangia are much elongated. *Plumularia lagenifera* is plumelike in appearance, from two to four inches high, and grows in clusters, with a simple stem and alternate hydrocladia which, unlike the preceding species, are not in the same plane. It occurs from Alaska to San Diego between tides to twenty-five fathoms.

Perhaps the most beautiful of the hydroids is the species *Aglaophenia struthionides*, popularly known as the Ostrich Plume. It is found along the Pacific coast and varies in size and color, with the stem reaching a height of three and a quarter inches. The hydrothecae are arranged in a single row on one side of each short branch, their margins or rims each with eleven sharp-pointed teeth, and each with three projecting nematophores. The Ostrich Plume occurs between tides to twenty-five fathoms.

12. The Trachomedusans

The trachomedusans are animals that lack a hydroid stage in most cases; where this stage is present, it is of minute size and more or less insignificant. The medusae, on the other hand, are usually rather large, more or less bell-shaped, with a velum, and four, six, or eight radial canals that bear the gonads on the subumbrella surface. The manubrium is usually quite long and often extends beyond the velum; the tentacles, too, are frequently very long. Specialized sense organs or lithocysts either freely project on the margin of the umbrella or are enclosed in pockets. In these animals alternation of generations appears for the most part to be absent, the medusae giving rise directly to other medusae instead of to hydroids. The trachomedusans are essentially open-sea animals, most of which are not tied to the shores by a hydroid generation. There are, however, exceptions as in the species of *Gonionemus*.

There are seven species of *Gonionemus* which are cosmopolitan in distribution, one species, *Gonionemus murbachi*, being common in Vineyard and Long Island Sounds. It is a beautiful and delicate little medusa or jellyfish with an umbrella about four-fifths of an inch in diameter and about half as high. The tentacles, three-quarters as long as the diameter of the bell, extend stiffly out on all sides, and number from sixty to eighty. They are armed with ringlike batteries of stinging cells. An adhesive pad equipped with nematocysts is present near the tip of each tentacle, beyond which the tentacle bends sharply to a right angle.

92

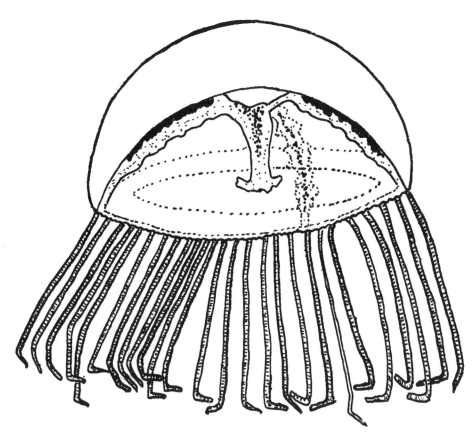

Gonionemus murbachi, medusa

The adhesive pads enable the medusa to cling to seaweeds and to various objects on the sea bottom. The manubrium is spindle-shaped and cruciform in cross section, with four frilled oral lobes that are whitish, the manubrium itself being dark brown tinged with pink. There are four straight radial canals extending from the manubrium to the bell margin, each bearing a much ruffled brown gonad which, if straightened out, would be longer than the radial canals. Numerous lithocysts are present and at the base of each tentacle there is a bright green pigment spot.

Like most medusae, *Gonionemus* does not merely float in the water but moves rhythmically up and down through a distance of several feet. It moves upward by repeated, slow, graceful contractions of the body, the contracting muscle fibers being arranged circularly just beneath the epidermis of the subumbrella surface of the umbrella, and also in the velum. By contracting, these muscles close the umbrella, and by the contraction of the velum the size of the opening beneath the umbrella is diminished and the animal is pushed upward by the downward jet of water thus produced. Between contractions the elasticity of the body re-opens the umbrella.

As the jellyfish is slightly heavier than sea water, downward movement is effected by the animal ceasing to swim, and thus sinking slowly. At such time the contracting muscles relax completely and the medusa opens wide. During ascent the tentacles are usually shortened by the contractions of the muscles running through them, but during descent these muscles also relax and the tentacles slowly elongate. As it sinks the jellyfish usually turns over, probably as a result of its shape. By thus alternately swimming up and sinking, *Gonionemus* is able to secure its food.

That the jellyfish is able to swim upward rather than at random is due to an orienting mechanism in the form of statocysts, sense structures that determine the direction of gravity. Each statocyst is a small concretion of calcium carbonate suspended in a flexible stalk in a cavity. The pressure of the concretion against the cells in the wall of the cavity appears to bring about orientation. The statocysts are embedded in the margin of the bell between the bases of the tentacles.

Unlike some species of medusae that have eyespots that serve to direct them toward or away from light, *Gonionemus* lacks such eyespots and yet it is affected by the intensity of light, sinking when the light is strong and rising when it is weak. The temperature and pH level of the water are other factors that seem to influence the average depth at which the medusa stays. Should the temperature or pH increase the jellyfish moves to greater depths, but should the temperature or pH decrease it rises toward the surface. At night when the light is less intense and the pH of the water falls slightly, it is found closer to the surface than during daytime.

Sense receptors that respond to temperature and pH are located around the margin of the umbrella, where are also located sense receptors to chemicals. If the juice of food organisms is added to the water, *Gonionemus* becomes quite active and swims about both horizontally and upward, at the same time keeping its tentacles extended in search of prey.

Once prey has been caught it is conveyed by the tentacles, as in the hydra, towards the mouth which is an opening at the end of the manubrium. At the same time the side of the umbrella holding the prey shrinks and bends inward while the manubrium extends and bends towards the prey. Four lips surround the mouth, each folded longi-

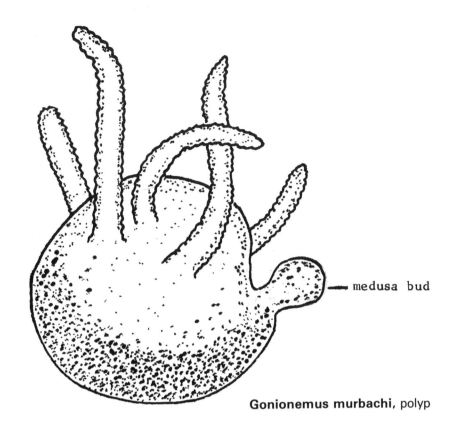

Gonionemus murbachi, polyp

tudinally, the inner side of the fold—toward the mouth—being ciliated. Mucus is secreted on this surface and the ciliary activity moves the mucous sheet steadily into the mouth. Once the lips have folded over the prey, the tentacles release their hold and the jellyfish resumes its normal shape.

When the jellyfish is not digesting food the mouth usually remains open, so that water enters through the mouth and is circulated throughout the gastrovascular system by the cilia that line the tracts. Hence all the tissues are usually in direct contact with sea water, thus promoting a direct exchange of gases and waste products by diffusion. During the process of digestion, when the mouth is closed, the water in the gastrovascular cavity doubtless contains enough oxygen to provide the animal with this necessary element until water again begins to circulate through it.

Both eggs and sperms are discharged into the surrounding water where fertilization takes place. The eggs develop into ciliated larvae, or planulae, which become attached to some solid object and become small, squat polyps. As these polyps grow they reproduce asexually by budding,

95

the buds eventually developing into typical polyps, but in the summer they produce spherical buds that develop into medusae.

One of the few freshwater coelenterates, *Craspedacusta ryderi* occurs in ponds and streams in various states such as Pennsylvania, Georgia, Kentucky, Ohio, Indiana, New Jersey, New York, Alabama, and Missouri. The hydroid is extremely minute and cylindrical in form, a simple tube attached at one end to sticks, stones, etc., without tentacles but with a crown of nematocysts around the mouth. It reproduces asexually by budding off individuals like itself. The medusae are budded off from one side and when full grown measure about one-half of an inch in diameter. They are disc-shaped, with four radial canals, a long manubrium, many tentacles, and numerous lithocysts.

Aglaura hemistoma is a cosmopolitan species, common in warm and tropical waters. The hydroid stage is wanting. The medusa is cylindrical or octagonal, the bell about one-quarter inch high in the female, about three-eighths in the male, with eight radial canals. The female has a circlet of from forty-eight to eighty-five rigid tentacles radiating from the bell margin with slightly club-shaped ends; the male has very short stub-like tentacles. The fingerlike gonads are suspended from the manubrium.

A beautiful and graceful medusa nearly one and a half inches high, *Aglantha digitale* is found in both the North Atlantic and North Pacific and is often common on the New England coast. It is elongate and mitre-shaped, the bell coming to a point at the top, with eighty to one hundred long, almost S-shaped brittle tentacles. The manubrium is spindle-shaped and extends from the apex of the subumbrella surface to the level of the bell margin, where it ends in a mouth having four everted lips. Eight long, slender gonads are attached to the eight radial canals and are suspended from the upper end of the subumbrella. The gonads are pale yellow, the tentacles pink, and the entire medusa is translucent and often displays iridescent colors. The hydroid stage is wanting, the eggs

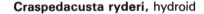

Craspedacusta ryderi, hydroid

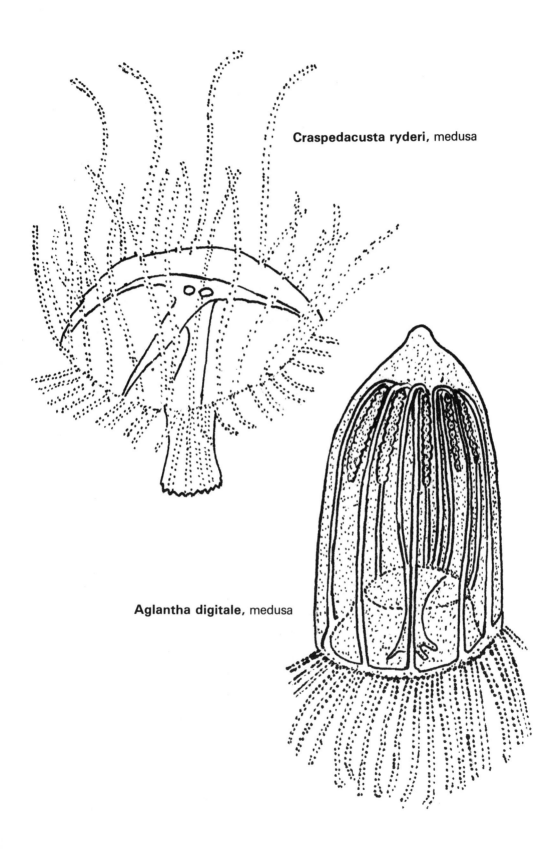

Craspedacusta ryderi, medusa

Aglantha digitale, medusa

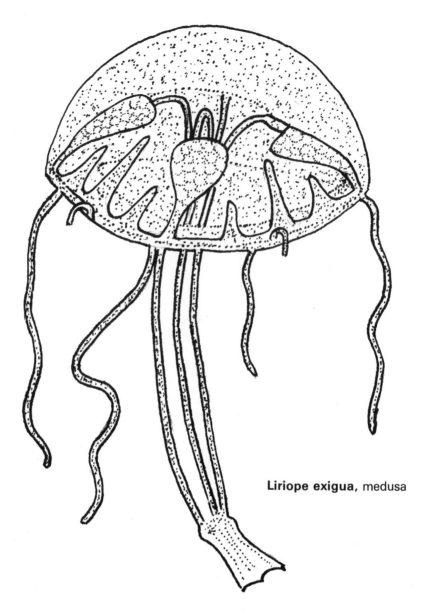

Liriope exigua, medusa

developing into a larva (actinula) which is transformed directly into the medusa.

Occurring throughout the warm parts of the Atlantic and the Mediterranean, *Liriope exigua* is a beautiful medusa about one-half inch in diameter. The bell is hemispherical, the manubrium extends far beyond the narrow velum and ends in a four-lobed trumpetlike mouth, the four tentacles are hollow and undulate from the margin on which there are four enclosed lithocysts, and a heart-shaped gonad is situated on each of

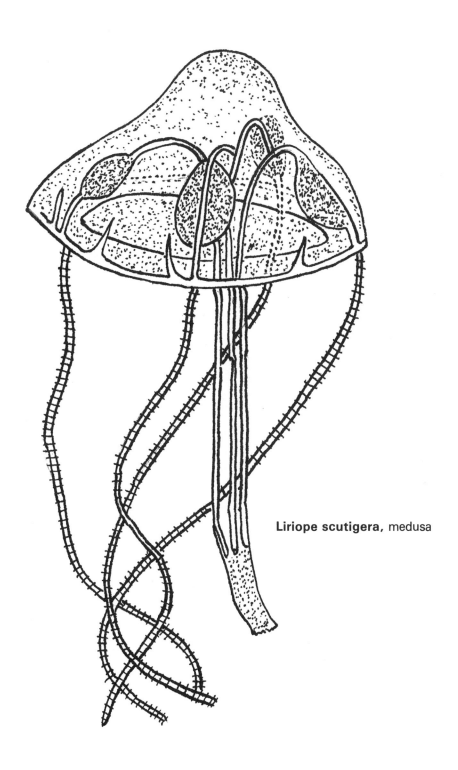

Liriope scutigera, medusa

the four radial canals, between each pair of which are one to three centri-petal canals, extending from the circular canal upwards. The gonads are rosy red in color, in some species green, and are quite conspicuous. There is no hydroid stage, the eggs developing into a larva that changes into the medusa. A related species, *Liriope scutigera*, very abundant along the Atlantic coast south of Cape Cod, has a bell with slightly sinuous sides that round into a flattened top. The medusa is about three-quarters of an inch in diameter, with four pink tentacles and a yellow manubrium that extends some distance beyond the bell and ends in a four-parted mouth. The gonads are oval, pale green, and are situated on the four radial canals.

13. The Narcomedusans

The narcomedusans are animals that live in the open ocean and lack a hydroid stage, the eggs hatching into larvae (actinulae) that transform directly into medusae. These have a lobed margin, stiff tentacles that extend from the exumbrella, and a gastrovascular cavity that is either circular in outline or has radial pouches or canals extending outwards. Sometimes a ring canal follows the marginal lobes and the umbrella is provided with freely projecting sensory clubs that arise from thickenings equipped with bristles. A ring at the edge of the umbrella has prolongations or cushionlike pads (peronia) that act as a support and that extend to the base of the tentacles. The gonads are situated on the subumbrella or along the radial canals.

A cosmopolitan species found in all tropical seas and quite common at Beaufort, North Carolina, *Cunoctantha octonaria* has a somewhat flattened bell with eight tentacles that project stiffly from its outer circumference, and that arise midway between the apex and the margin. They have very little motion but are amply provided with stinging cells. The adult medusae have twenty-four sense organs, each set upon a small elevation of the bell margin. The velum, consisting of a ring-shaped membrane, extends upwards as eight wedge-shaped webs. The manubrium is cone-shaped and ends in a four-lipped mouth. The jellyfish is transparent with tinges of green near the tentacles. The larvae live

Cunoctantha octonaria, medusa

parasitically in the bell of the mother where they produce other larvae like themselves by budding.

Another narcomedusan, *Cunina lativentris*, occurs in the Atlantic Ocean and in the Mediterranean Sea. The medusa is flat, transparent, about five-eighths of an inch in diameter, and has ten to twelve tentacles, marginal lobes, and gastrovascular pouches, with four lithocysts on each lobe. A third species, found along the Pacific coast, is *Aegina rosea*. The medusa is bell-shaped with a diameter of two to five inches and four to six tentacles, the tentacles and cavity yellow or rose-red.

14. The Scypho-medusans

Probably no animals along our coasts excite as much interest and attention as the jellyfishes. These unique animals, in their transparency and with their graceful rhythmical movements and long streaming tentacles, are always fascinating to watch and a source, too, of some wonder as to how such seemingly delicate animals can withstand the buffetings of the sea.

The name jellyfish is a misnomer, for these animals are not fishes nor are they made of jelly; actually they consist of ninety-nine percent of water. As we have already seen, they are also known as medusae because of their long tentacles that suggest the locks of the mythological Gorgon. The jellyfishes and medusae of the preceding pages are all small forms; the larger species, which many consider to be the true jellyfishes, are known as the scyphomedusans. The scyphomedusans differ from the hydromedusans in that the medusae lack a velum, and there are various other differences.

Jellyfishes vary considerably in size, from that of a pinhead to as much as six or seven feet in diameter. They also differ in the number, size, and position of the tentacles, in the number of the radial canals, and in the form of the manubrium, but their internal structure is much the same in all species. These odd animals have been likened to the mushroom in shape, the cap and stalk of the mushroom being represented by the umbrella and manubrium of the jellyfish.

The scyphomedusans usually have an alternation of generations, though in some species there is only the medusoid generation while in others only the hydroid stage is present. The latter is a small, generally non-colonial animal, less than half an inch high, that resembles the Hydra in appearance but differs from it in having an ectodermal gullet and four longitudinal folds of the endoderm called mesenteries, which project into the gastrovascular cavity. Also, the aboral end (the end opposite the mouth) is fixed or attached to the sea bottom or to some object in a cup formed of the perisarc. The hydroid is called a scyphistoma and is an asexual animal, reproducing exclusively by budding. New scyphistomas are produced by the budding of stolons sent off from the foot, the medusae or jellyfishes by a process of terminal budding called strobilation. In the latter instance, as the scyphistoma grows it becomes constricted at intervals, the constrictions dividing into a number of discs which resembles as pile of inverted saucers with lobed edges. Each of the discs is called an ephyra and is a young medusa or jellyfish which, on being set free, eventually grows into a sexual animal.

The medusae vary in size and have the margin of the bell lobed or scalloped, usually with eight notches. They may or may not have tentacles. In some species that manubrium is very long, large, and extensively branched, and in some species the mouth is closed by a coalescence of its sides but with small pores through which food is taken. The gastrovascular cavity is complex in form and usually consists of four radial pouches that form a large space in the middle of the animal.

The medusae have four gonads which are often brightly colored. In many species the subumbrella contains, directly beneath the four gonads, four large pockets called the subgenital pockets. They appear to be respiratory in function. There are usually also a number of cylindrical filaments beside each gonad, which are equipped with stinging cells.

In the scyphomedusans the mesoglea differs from that of the hydromedusans in that it is usually cellular and hence firmer. The sense organs, too, differ and are modified tentacles, being called tentaculocysts or rhopalia.

There are some 200 species of true jellyfishes and they are all marine. They are carnivorous in food habits, feeding on small organisms such as crustaceans and even fishes. Their life span usually does not exceed a year. Being almost entirely composed of water, those thrown upon the beaches by storms and high tides rapidly disappear, leaving no trace behind. The large medusae are formidable creatures with their stinging cells and can be a serious menace to bathers. Doubtless some drownings may be attributed to swimmers having been paralyzed by them.

The most common jellyfish occurring along both our coasts is the species *Aurelia aurita*, popularly known as the Moon Jellyfish or White Sea Jelly. It may often be seen on a beach, cast there by a storm or high tide. In color it is a translucent milky white, or bluish with pink or white gonads.

The body of the adult medusa is flat and disc-like and measures from six to ten inches in diameter, but when swimming it varies from hemispherical to a more or less flattened disc. The tentacles are many in number; they are short and fringelike and completely surround the disc a

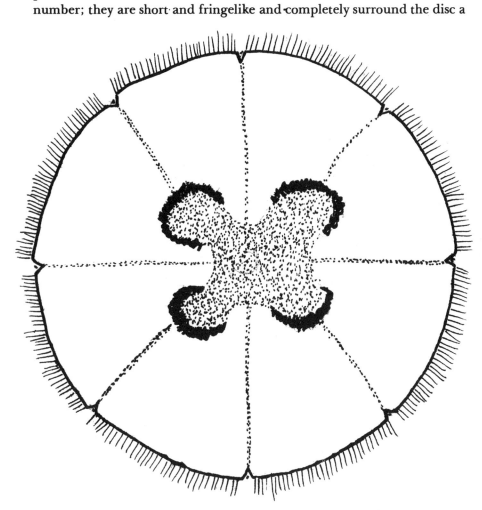

Moon Jellyfish or White Sea Jelly, **Aurelia aurita**

little above the margin, alternating with the same number of tiny lappets. The mouth is four-sided with four long, narrow, somewhat tapering lobes. There are four large subgenital pockets and eight rhopalia in as many marginal indentations. The four radial canals are narrow and branching and form a complex system with the circular canal connecting the distal ends. The four gonads are conspicuous in a horseshoe shape around the center of the disc. They are pink in the male, white in the female.

The medusae swim in shoals and are common in summer. They may be considered as annual animals as they appear regularly as free-swimming jellyfishes in the latter part of April. At this time they may be seen in large numbers near the surface from the deck of a ship when the water is smooth and the sky is clear. They are about an inch in diameter but grow rapidly and by the end of June have attained their full size. By the end of July they are fully developed and the female medusae begin to discharge their eggs into the gastrovascular cavity, where they are fertilized by the sperms that have been liberated through the mouth of the male medusae and have entered the cavity with the food currents. After being fertilized the eggs enter the lobes around the mouth where they remain until they have become planulae. When freed, the planulae become attached to

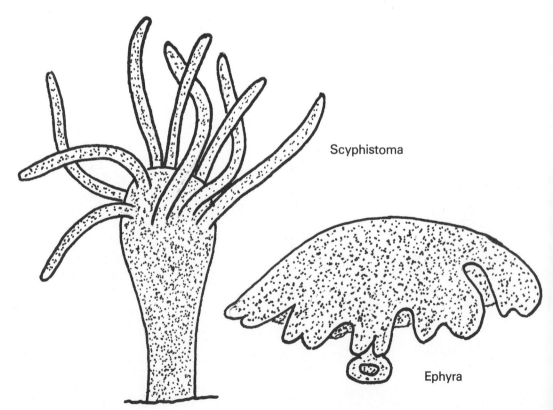

Scyphistoma

Ephyra

rocks and seaweeds of the shore where they develop into scyphistomas. During the winter these grow and divide into ephyrae that are set free in April.

After spawning, the medusae, reduced in strength and unable to resist the storms of autumn, are cast ashore or are so weakened that they become easy victims to the small crustaceans that gather in swarms to attack and destroy them.

A magnificent species more than seven inches in diameter, *Stomolophus meleagris* occurs along the coast from Florida to North Carolina, occasionally to New England, and along the coast of southern California,

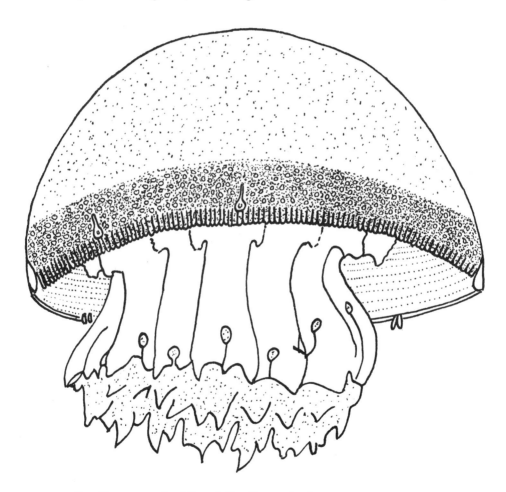

The Many-mouthed Sea Jelly, **Stomolophus meleagris**

and is often quite common. The body is hemispherical, brown in color, and strangely resembles a cone-capped mushroom. There are eight oral lobes with sucking pores along their edges which take the place of the mouth, hence the popular name of this species as the Many-mouthed Sea Jelly. The lobes are fused to form a thick cylinder, at the bottom of which are eight pairs of frilled lobes. There are eight marginal sense organs or rhopalia with sense-clubs deeply set within the niches between the lappets, the sense-clubs hollow and slender-shaped with knoblike ends containing pigmented concretions. There are some 128 lappets and sixteen radial canals that give off a network of branches throughout the umbrella.

The species *Rhopilema verrilli* is also hemispherical and much larger in size, often attaining a diameter of a foot or more. There are eight separated, three-winged oral lobes with multitudes of sucking pores from which numerous club-shaped filaments are suspended. Although not common, this species may be readily seen because of its yellowish color. It occurs from Long Island Sound southwards. A related species, *Rhopilema esculenta*, is the edible jellyfish of China and Japan.

The little iridescent jellyfish known as the Stalked Scyphomedusan, *Lucernaria quadricornis* is commonly found attached to seaweeds and eelgrass by a stalk-like projection of the top of the umbrella. This and some other twenty or more related species are generally considered to be undeveloped or degenerate medusae which remain as scyphistomas. They are, in other words, undeveloped medusae that are attached upside down by an extension of the umbrella with the mouth pointing upward.

The bell of the Stalked Scyphomedusan is quadrangular in shape, about two inches or more in diameter, and about two and a half inches in height. The margin has eight prominent lobes, the summit of each crowned with pompons of more than a hundred tentacles. The gastro-vascular cavity has four pouches lined by eight gonads. The species is extremely variable in color and may be green, gray, or reddish. It is widely distributed on the coasts of Europe, Greenland, and North America north of Cape Cod.

Another stalked species is *Haliclystus auricula*. It is somewhat smaller than the preceding, being about an inch wide and an inch high. The stalk is four-sided and the bell margin is right-sided or with eight marginal lobes and as many notches, the lobes ending in clusters of hollow, knobby tentacles. In the angles between the lobes there is an adhesive pad which may function as an anchor. The color of this species, which occurs from Cape Cod to Greenland, and along the northern coasts of Europe and Alaska, is quite variable, various individuals being blue, green, yellow, olive, orange, red, pink, or violet.

A jellyfish that is remarkable for its high, narrowly pointed bell with gracefully curving sides is the species *Periphylla hyacinthina*, popularly known as the Lappet-bordered Jellyfish, so named from its sixteen marginal lobes or lappet pouches. The bell may be nearly five inches in diameter and more than six inches in height. There is a constriction about the middle, and twelve tentacles are inserted high up in the notches, in a series of three each between four lappets. Four sense organs are located in notches which are not as deeply cut as the other twelve. Within the umbrella cavity there are four funnel-shaped interradial pits or subgenital pockets. They are set against the stomach and extend along its sides almost to the apex of the umbrella. There are eight horseshoe-shaped gonads. A purple color lines the inside of the umbrella, the sense organs are brown, and the tentacles and lappets a translucent light blue.

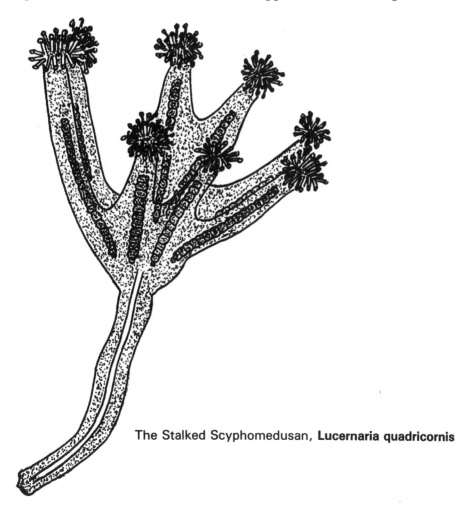

The Stalked Scyphomedusan, **Lucernaria quadricornis**

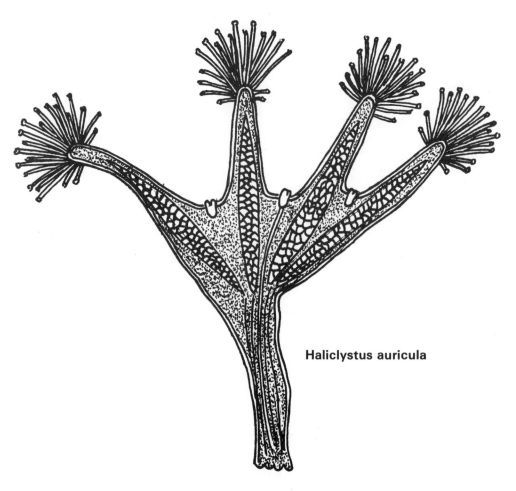

Haliclystus auricula

The Lappet-bordered Jellyfish is cosmopolitan in distribution; along our Atlantic coast it occurs from the Bay of Biscay to Cape Hatteras, where it may often be seen swimming on the surface of the water.

The Four-sided Jellyfish, *Tamoya haplonema*, is so named from the flattened sides of the umbrella which give it a quadrangular appearance. This jellyfish has four interradial tentacles, the bases of which are expanded to form prominent flattened structures or leaflike spines called pedalia. Midway between the pedalia, the umbrella margin is notched to enclose a sense organ (rhopalium). A false velum (velarium) is present, which with the energetic swimming movements of the animal gives it the appearance of being a hydromedusan. The stomach is large and deep and occupies almost the entire cavity of the bell. In the four gastric canals the plate-like gonads extend downward to the tentacle bases like frilled curtains. The bell is quite transparent and along the margin are clusters

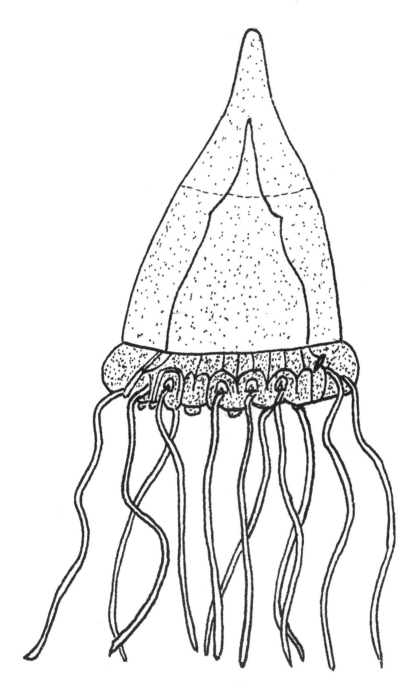

The Lappet-bordered Jellyfish, **Periphylla hyacinthina**

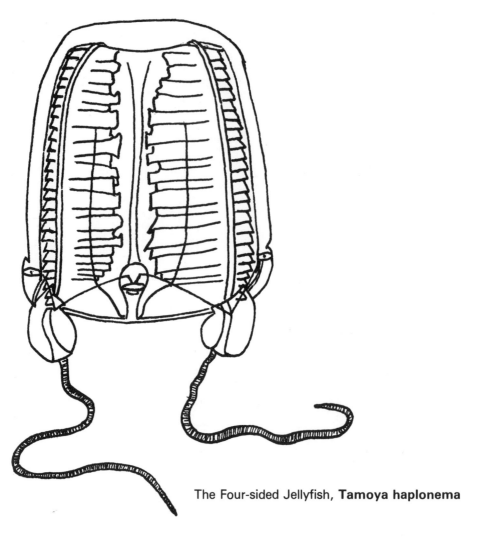

The Four-sided Jellyfish, **Tamoya haplonema**

of stinging cells. The Four-sided Jellyfish is abundant from Long Island Sound southwards throughout the West Indies to Brazil.

Perhaps the most distinguishing feature of the species *Chiropsalmus quadrumanus* are the four groups of about eight tentacles each, each group extending from the fingers of a handlike pedalium. The tentacles are very flexible and are equipped with numerous stinging cells. The bell is about four inches high and about five and a half inches wide. From four radially situated pouches, finger-shaped extensions project into the cavity of the bell. This jellyfish is erratically distributed from North Carolina southwards and is sometimes common in shallow water.

The bell of the Luminous Furbelowed Jellyfish, *Pelagia cyanella*, is very active during motion, becoming alternately globular and flattened.

The outer surface of the bell or exumbrella is covered with warts of nettle cells which radiate from the apex toward the margin of the umbrella. They are orange-red in color and so numerous as to appear as dotted lines. There are sixteen marginal lobes, and eight tentacles extend from alternate notches between them; rhopalia occupy the intervening notches. The mouth is quadrangular and projects below the margin of the bell. It has four long oral lobes, often folded and frilled, which serve as sensitive palps. The stomach is lens-shaped, with simple radial pouches that extend under the umbrella. There is no hydroid stage, the free-swimming adult medusa developing directly from the planula. The bell of this jellyfish is purple-rose, shading into blue, and is luminescent at night. It is one of the most beautiful of the medusae, and occurs from

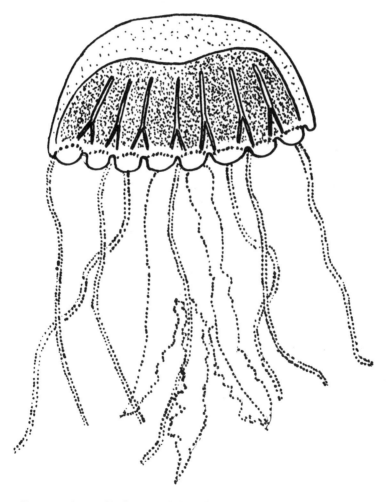

The Luminous Furbelowed Jellyfish, **Pelagia cyanella**

Cape Cod southwards to Brazil, as well as the Mediterranean where it is very abundant.

Another beautiful medusa with a bell that may reach nearly eight inches in diameter is the Golden-fringed Furbelowed Jellyfish, *Dactylometra quinquecirrha*. As in the preceding species, small wartlike clusters of stinging cells are scattered over the umbrella, most numerous at the apex. There are forty-eight marginal lobes, eight marginal sense organs or rhopalia, and forty golden yellow tentacles that stream down for a considerable distance through the water. The mouth is quadrangular with four flounce-like oral lobes of rosy pink. This species is found from Long Island and Vineyard Sound southwards to the tropics.

The bell of the species *Nausithoë punctata* is literally a flattened one, the apex being less than a quarter of an inch high. The diameter is about half an inch. A deep furrow separates the disc of the bell from the encircling zone of sixteen lobes with their large convex pedalia. The pedalia alternate with each other in having a tentacle or a sense organ, the tentacles extending out abruptly from the margin of the bell. The mouth has four lips and looks like a cross, between the arms of which are four groups of cirri. The jellyfish varies in color from green to light brown, the umbrella having reddish spots, and the gonads being brown, red, or yellow. It is cosmopolitan in distribution, found floating on the surface in all tropical and warm seas, and is quite common, but occurs only occasionally north of Cape Hatteras.

The largest of our jellyfishes is the species *Cyanea capillata*, popularly known under the various names of the Great Pink Jellyfish, the Sun Jelly, the Sea Blubber, and the Lion's Mane. The disc is usually four to twelve inches in diameter, but many specimens have been seen with a diameter of as much as three feet and with tentacles seventy-five feet long when fully extended. Individuals about a foot in diameter are quite common along our coast. Extremely large specimens may attain a diameter of eight feet while their numerous long-trailing tentacles, as many as 800 in number, may be 200 feet in length when fully extended. The tentacles, instead of arising at the margin, are in clusters situated some distance back and extend from the subumbrella. Radiating from the gastrovascular cavity are numerous pouches which are very wide and give rise at their ends to branching canals. The oral lobes are very long, wide, and voluminous. Between the lobes and the tentacles are four large bunches of gonads. They are situated on the subumbrella floor on the four sides of the stomach, which is quadrangular in shape. The margin of the umbrella is cleft into eight main lobes, each of which in turn is partly divided by a median cleft with two shallow notches on either side of it, thus making thirty-two lobes divided by indentations. Eight marginal club-shaped sense organs are located at the innermost point of the eight median notches. The color of the umbrella varies from light yellow to brown, the gastrovascular cavity varies from a rosy pink to brownish-purple, the oral lobes are a rich brownish-purple, and the gonads and tentacles are yellow to reddish-brown. Sometimes individuals are bright pink or purplish.

This large and remarkable jellyfish is common from North Carolina northwards to the Arctic Ocean. It attains its largest size in the colder waters, those found south of Cape Cod being comparatively small. The species also occurs off the Pacific coast. Frequently the jellyfish may be found stranded on New England beaches, where it hardly suggests its beautiful appearance when floating in the water. A light-brown variety called *Cyanea fulva* occurs in Long Island Sound and a bluish-white variety, *Cyanea versicolor*, off the Carolina coast.

The large size of this jellyfish with its many tentacles and thousands of stinging cells makes it a formidable creature to encounter in the open sea. Swimmers are known to have died from the effect of coming in contact with the stinging power of its nematocysts.

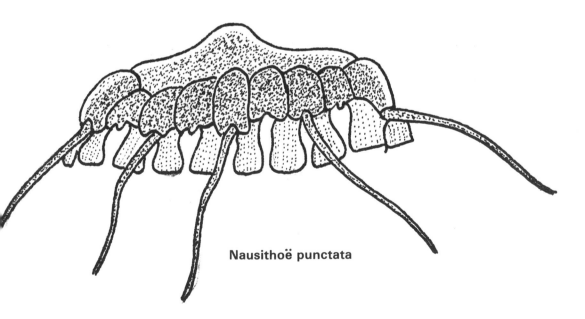

Nausithoë punctata

115

15. The Anthozoans

The anthozoans are the sea anemones, corals, sea pens, sea feathers, etc. These animals do not have a free-swimming medusa generation, the polyp form alone being present. The body is usually cylindrical in shape and is either permanently or temporarily attached at one end. The opposite end is flattened and is called the oral disc. The mouth, in the center of this disc, is surrounded by hollow tentacles of which there may be from six to several hundred. The mouth is not round, as might be expected, but is an elongated slit. A ciliated groove, called the siphonoglyph, is present at one or both ends.

Unlike the mouth of the hydromedusans which leads directly into the gastrovascular cavity, that of the anthozoans leads instead into a tube lined with ectoderm called the gullet or stomodaeum, which opens into the gastrovascular cavity below. This cavity is divided into a number of chambers that communicate with one another by six or more wide longitudinal ridges called mesenteries. These arise from the body wall and project towards the center of the cavity, though certain ones in the upper part of the body connect with the wall of the gullet, thus forming small chambers which are continued above in the hollow tentacles. But in the lower part of the cavity the edges of the mesenteries are free with convoluted thickening called the mesenterial filaments which contain the gonads and also stinging cells. In the sea anemones there are also long threads called acontia that are equipped with nematocysts and can be protruded through the siphonoglyph and, in some instances, through pores (cinclides) in the wall.

116

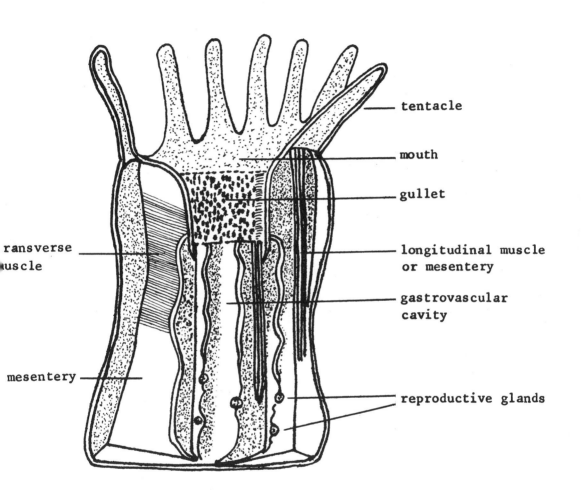

tentacle

mouth

gullet

ransverse
uscle

longitudinal muscle
or mesentery

gastrovascular
cavity

mesentery

reproductive glands

Longitudinal section of an anthozoan polyp

117

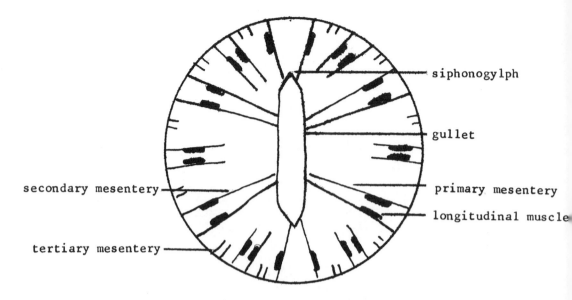

Cross section of an anthozoan

On the walls of the mesenteries are muscular bands known as longitudinal (retractor) muscles. In the sea anemones these muscles by contracting draw down the body of the animal, and at the same time retract the tentacles so that they may be concealed within the body. At the upper end of the body there is usually a sphincter muscle which draws this end together and closes the mouth. The body wall consists of two main layers of cells, the ectoderm and the endoderm, and between them the mesoglea which is, unlike that of the hydromedusans, cellular.

Most anthozoans have a characteristic skeleton composed either of calcium carbonate or of a hornlike substance called ceratine. Both are secreted by the ectoderm and function in elevating the colony in the water so that it can be brought into a position favorable to its existence.

In most instances the anthozoans are unisexual. The eggs and sperms are liberated into the gastrovascular cavity where partial development may take place. The fertilized eggs develop into planulae (both the eggs and sperms being expelled through the siphonoglyph) which after a short free life settle to the bottom, in most cases becoming fixed, and then develop into adult animals. Budding is also very general, leading to colony formation which is characteristic of the anthozoans.

The anthozoans are all marine animals and are especially abundant in the warmer seas. There are over 6000 living and many fossil species.

118

16. The Alcyonarians

The anthozoans fall naturally into two groups, those having eight tentacles, the alcyonarians, and those not having eight tentacles, the zoantharians.

The alcyonarians are colonial anthozoans that, in addition to having eight pinnate or branched tentacles, also have eight mesenteries and only one siphonoglyph, though this may be wanting in some species; it occurs, when present, on but one side of the polyp. The retractor muscles are all on one side of the mesenteries, that which faces the siphonoglyph. The skeleton, which in a few genera is lacking, consists either of calcium carbonate or ceratine spicules embedded in the mesoglea, the latter, thus reinforced by the spicules, together with the outer ectoderm, being called the *coenenchyma*. Depressions (calicles) in the coenenchyma contain the polyps, into which they can usually retract, and which are in communication with each other by means of canals. There are over 2,000 living species, many of which are brightly colored and phosphorescent and thus conspicuous objects in the warmer seas.

17. The Alcyonaceans

The alcyonaceans are alcyonarians having a skeleton of calcareous spicules of irregular shape embedded in the mesoglea In some instances the spicules are united into a branched axis but generally they are loosely enclosed in the mesoglea.

In the colonial species, *Cornulariella modesta*, the polyps are from one-fourth to three-fourths of an inch high and about one-eighth or an inch in diameter. They rise from a membranous or ribbonlike stolon and are not joined together except by the creeping stolon. They are seated in more or less rigid cups (calicles) into which they may be retracted. The stolons and the walls of the cups consist of strong spiny spicules that are closely packed together. The lower part of the polyps and the stolons are yellow or brown; the tentacles, long and tapering, are white. This alcyonarian occurs off the coasts of New Brunswick, Nova Scotia, and Maine in depths of thirty-five to a hundred fathoms.

Often dredged up by fishermen in 150 to 300 fathoms of water off the coasts of Nova Scotia and Newfoundland, the species *Anthomastus grandiflorus*, grows in large mushroom clusters that have a thick expanding stalk surmounted by many large polyps. The colony may be from three to five inches in diameter, the individual polyps as much as an inch in diameter.

A remarkably handsome species, *Gersemia carnea*, is pale flesh or salmon color, varying to light orange or pale red. It grows to a height of five inches and is very much branched. It occurs on stony or shelly

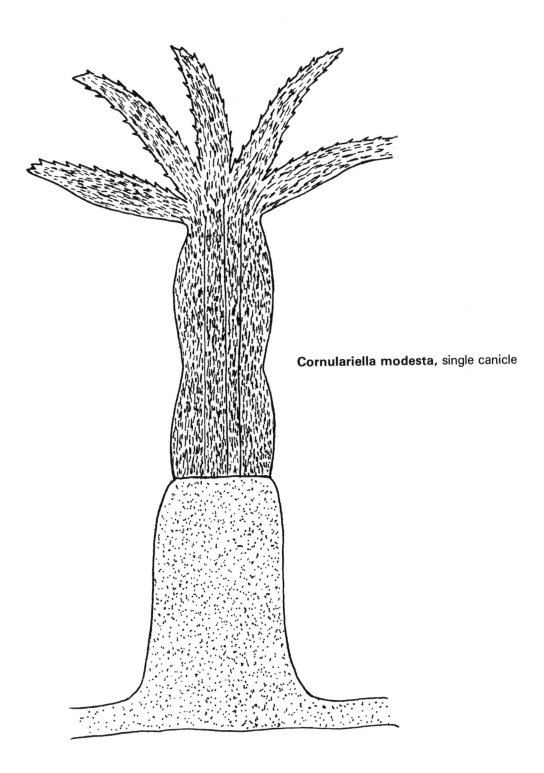

Cornulariella modesta, single canicle

121

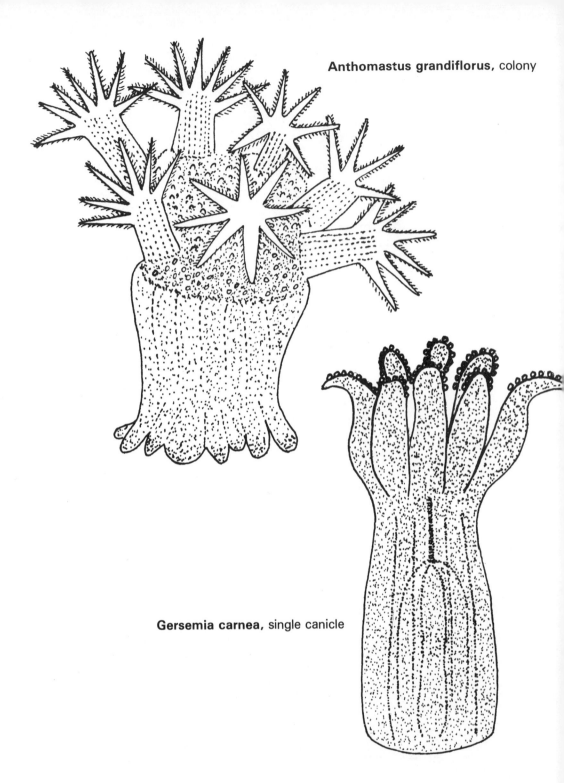

Anthomastus grandiflorus, colony

Gersemia carnea, single canicle

122

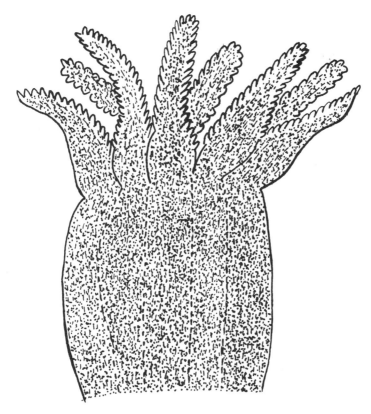

Gersemia rubiformis, single canicle

bottoms in ten to thirty fathoms, from the Gulf of St. Lawrence to Block Island, and is rather common.

Another species of the same genus, *Gersemia rubiformis* is a red-colored branching colonial alcyonacean with pear-shaped clusters of lobes. Its main stem has a thick covering of red spicules, except near the base, the surface thus having the appearance of being finely granular. This is an arctic species.

A large treelike species, *Duva multiflora*, which is light red to pink in color, when fully developed may be as much as four and a half inches high and three inches in diameter. The large smooth stalk has numerous branches, with the polyps crowded in clusters at their tips. When the polyps are contracted they look cauliflower-like, hence the popular name of the species, the Sea Cauliflower. It is rather common in depths of 130 fathoms or more off Nova Scotia and Newfoundland.

Drifa glomerata is an upright colony, pale red in color, shaded toward brown on the stalk and with translucent yellow or orange polyps. It has a

123

Duva multiflora, segment of colony

stout trunk with branches from all sides. These are rather conical in shape and have crowded clusters of three to twelve polyps. The species is abundant on the Newfoundland banks.

A very common species that grows in closely branched, bushlike colonies a foot or less high is the species *Acanella normani,* having the popular name of Bush Coral from its manner of branching. The branches, often set at a wide angle to the stalk, are snakelike in appearance, with the stouter branches at the bottom of the stalk. The calicles are elongated and closely set in whorls around the branches. Each has a cylinder of eight spines at the crown. The colony is light chestnut brown, varying to orange and dark brown, the main axis being white with orange-brown nodes. It is abundant in deep water off the banks of Nova Scotia and Newfoundland.

An unusual type of colony formation occurs in the species *Radicipes*

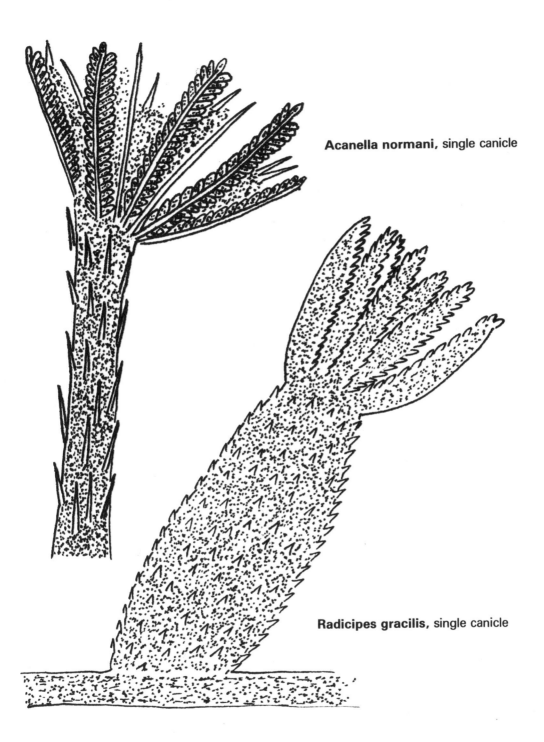

Acanella normani, single canicle

Radicipes gracilis, single canicle

125

gracilis which grows in the form of tall, slender rodlike stems that extend upward for three feet or more from a branching rootlike base. A delicate crust composed of thin, oblong spicules resembling scales covers the axis, from which the calicles of the polyps bud off obliquely and which are well separated from each other. The calicles are orange, sometimes with a pinkish cast. The species occurs off Georges Bank where it is often dredged up.

The Gold-banded Coral, *Keratoisis ornata*, found in depths of 200 to 300 fathoms on the banks of Nova Scotia, is an irregular branching colony with a slender, gradually tapering form, sometimes over four feet high, with ivory white calcareous joints that are usually longitudinally grooved and very finely granular. The calicles are large and conspicuous and look almost like a series of elongated tumblers crowned with eight projecting spines.

Abundant off the Grand Banks, *Lepidomuricea grandis* is more or less fanlike in its growth, all the branches being practically in one plane. The calicles are cylindrical, sometimes conical, with their margins protected by one or two rows of sharp-pointed spines. The spines of the tentacles form a V-shaped pattern.

The species *Acanthogorgia armata* is a profusely branching colony with a horny and fibrous axis that gives it a sort of rough appearance. The calicles are elongated, cylindrical, and spiny, and are profusely and irregularly sessile on all the branches, sometimes being crowded close together. The spicules are spindle-shaped and are so arranged that they form eight spiny ridges on the outside of the calicle which end in as many sawlike extensions surrounding the opening of the cup, thus appearing much like a delicate coronet. This species occurs in fairly deep water along the Atlantic coast.

The colony of *Alcyonium carneum*, the Yellowish-red Coral, so named because of its color, is composed of short, thick lobes with long polyps which, except for the outer end with the tentacles, are entirely buried in the mass of the coenenchyma which forms the bulk of the colony, and which is provided with numerous spicules. The species is one and a half to four inches high and occurs from low water to eighty fathoms, from Long Island Sound to the Gulf of St. Lawrence.

The species *Alcyonium digitatum* is known by the unpleasant name of Dead Man's Fingers because of a fancied resemblance to a human hand with only the stumps of the fingers. As in the preceding species, the bulk of the colony is a mass of coenenchyma which contains scattered spicules

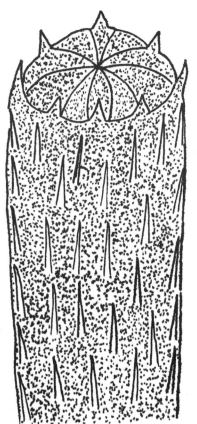

The Gold-banded Coral, **Keratoisis ornata,** single canicle

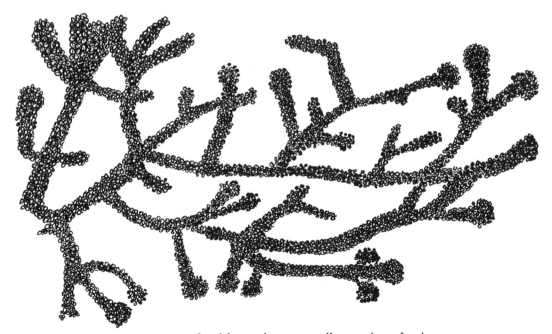

Lepidomuricea grandis, section of colony

that give it rigidity. When the polyps are fully extended, the colony is rather attractive in appearance, but not so when contracted. This colony is found sometimes at low-water mark but usually in deeper water, attached to shells and stones. It is abundant on the New England coast.

The familiar Organ-pipe Coral, *Tubipora spp.*, is so named because of its peculiar manner of growth which resembles a series of organ pipes. It is found in the East Indian seas and is deep red in color and very fragile, consisting of many tubes slightly separated from one another but connected by horizontal platforms at short intervals. The spicules of calcium carbonate secreted in the polyp are united or fused into a tube or cylindrical skeleton. During certain stages of development, the polyps send out horizontal expansions which unite and become calcified, forming the shelf which binds the tubes together. From the top of the platforms other corallites are formed, and thus a colony is made, which broadens as it rises in its growth.

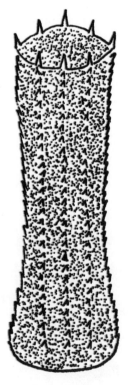

Acanthogorgia armata, single canicle

128

18. The Gorgonaceans

The gorgonaceans are alcyonarians that have a firm and usually much branched axis. The axis, composed of compacted spicules, may be either calcareous or hornlike, or may consist of alternating calcareous and hornlike segments; it is covered with a rind of coenenchyma containing spicules in which the polyps are embedded and which are connected by endodermal canals. The animals are popularly known as the sea fans and sea whips. There are about a thousand species.

The Sea Fan, *Gorgonia flabellum*, is typical of the species. It is an erect, branching, treelike colony, up to twenty inches high, and as wide, the branches in the same plane or fanlike and forming a network with meshes 1/8" to 1/4" wide, the central supporting axis of a flexible horny material so that the colony can sway gracefully with the currents of water. The polyps are minute and retractile and the entire colony is yellowish or reddish in color. The species occurs in shallow water in the South Atlantic and the West Indies.

A related species, *Gorgonia acerosa*, is also treelike, with long, slender branches, the smaller branches being arranged pinnately or feather-fashion. It grows to a height of thirty inches, is straw colored, and like the preceding species is also found in shallow water in the West Indies.

A third gorgonacean occurring in the West Indies is *Eunicea crassa*. The colony is treelike with cylindrical trunks and grows up to twenty inches high. The axis is hornlike, the coenenchyma is thick and corky,

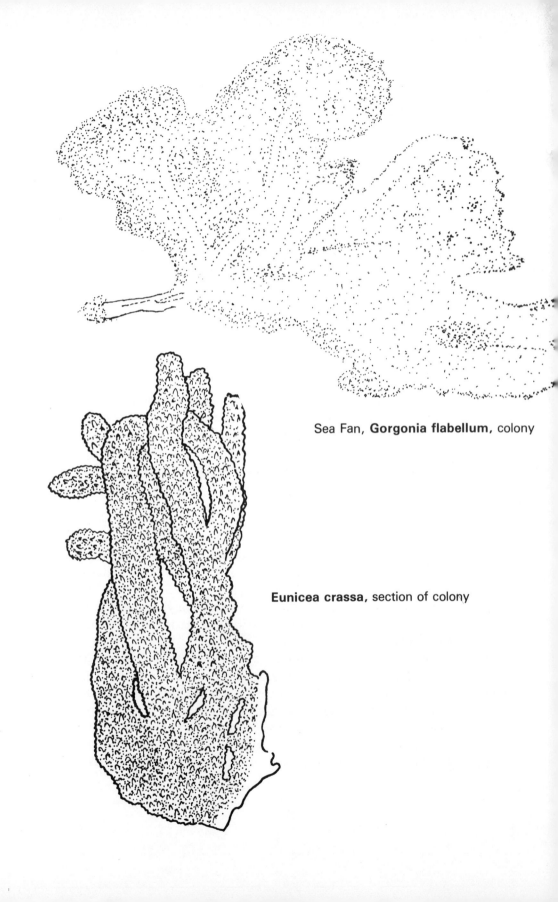

Sea Fan, **Gorgonia flabellum,** colony

Eunicea crassa, section of colony

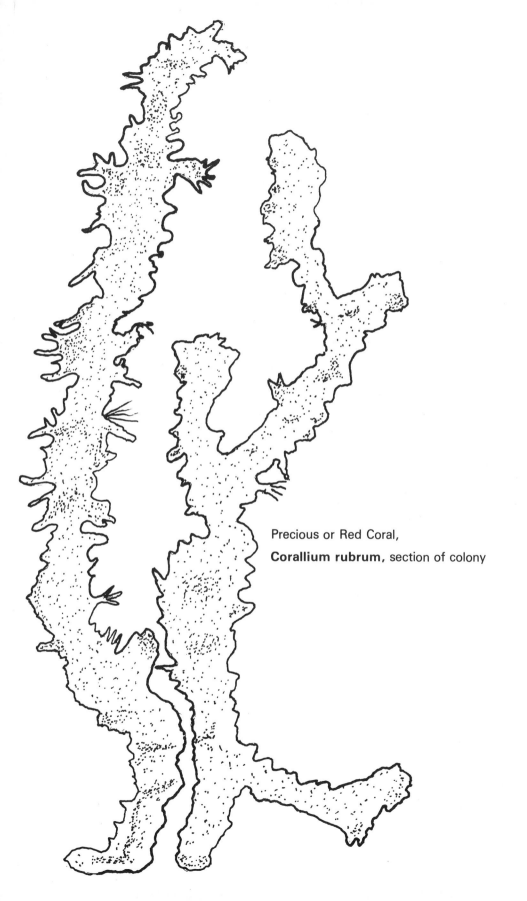

Precious or Red Coral,

Corallium rubrum, section of colony

and the polyps, which are large and projecting with bilobed or crenate edges, are scattered over the entire surface.

A very common West Indies species, *Plexaurella dichotoma*, is treelike with cylindrical trunks, a horny axis, a thick coenenchyma, and smooth club-shaped branches. The species is brownish in color.

The Precious or Red Coral of commerce, *Corallium rubrum*, used extensively in jewelry, is a member of this group of alcyonarians. It is an erect, branching colony up to a foot high, with a dense red calcareous axis and fused red spicules, the axis thick, longitudinally ridged by endodermal canals, and extremely hard. The slender branches, when broken, make the beads so familiar to everyone. The polyps are white in color and are retractile. The Precious Coral is found in the central and western Mediterranean and is fished principally off the coast of Italy and Africa. Other species of the genus occur in the Atlantic Ocean and in Japanese waters, but they are not used as extensively for jewelry.

The sea fans and sea whips range from the Antarctic to the Arctic and from shallow to abyssal depths. They are named from their forms: some have shapes which resemble branching shrubs, others are long branched rods, either straight or spiral. In great variety they grow in abundance on the coral reefs and mud-flats of Florida where they form masses of low shrubbery, pink, yellow, brown, or purple in color.

19. The Pennatulaceans

The pennatulaceans are alcyonarians that are popularly known as the sea pens and sea feathers because their singular colonies resemble the quill-feathers once used as writing pens. The colonies are not fixed but are capable of independent movement. They consist of two parts, a stalk, which may be embedded in the sand or mud of the sea bottom, and an upper part called the rachis, which bears the polyps. It has plumelike branches or pinnae and may have the form of a feather, a rod, or a broad plate. A central axis is usually present which may be either calcareous or hornlike, its outer layers in the form of a crust in which many spicules are embedded. The polyps communicate with one another by means of endo-dermal canals, and are of two forms: large polyps with the usual structure called autozooids, these being the feeding polyps, and smaller polyps without tentacles, gonads, or mesenteries, called siphonozooids, their function being to control or regulate the inflow and outflow of water throughout the canals of the animal. There are over 300 species. They occur at moderate depths and are widely distributed.

One of the more common — and beautiful and graceful — species is popularly known as the Red Sea Pen, *Pennatula aculeata*. It is four inches long, the rachis having paired lateral leaves or pinnae that number from twenty to fifty on each side and bear the autozooids on their upper margin. The siphonozooids are on the under side of the rachis and there

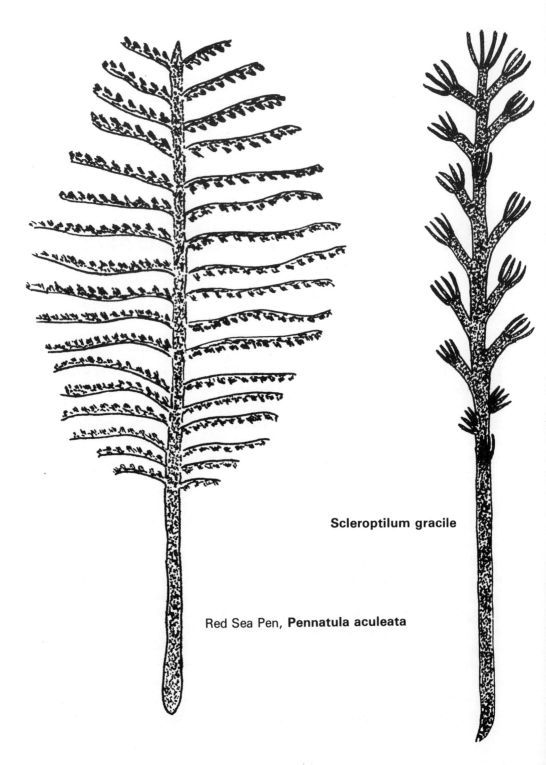

Scleroptilum gracile

Red Sea Pen, **Pennatula aculeata**

are numerous spines among them. The plumelike pinnae range in color from deep red to purplish-red and the stalk is pale orange or yellow. There are also pink and rose-colored varieties, as well as albinos. The Red Sea Pen occurs from Nova Scotia to the Carolinas, as well as along the coast of Europe, in sixty to a thousand fathoms, being more abundant in deep water. It is often brought in by fishermen from the various fishing banks.

A much larger species, the Great Sea Pen, *Pennatula borealis*, often

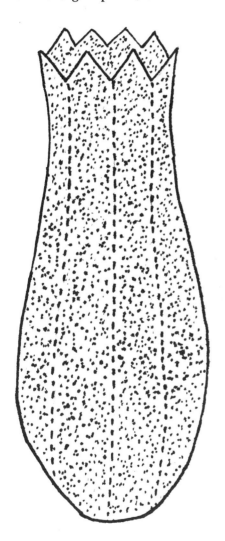

Funiculina armata, single canicle

attains a length of twenty inches and a width of five to six inches. Near the top of the stalk there is a strong, bulbous, muscular enlargement. This enlargement is usually orange-red to purplish-red, the lower part of the stalk varying from yellowish to orange. The edges of the pinnae are the same color as the enlargement while the parts of the pinnae near the stalk are the same color as the lower part of the stalk. The siphonozooids are usually very many and are red in color. This species occurs from Newfoundland to Nantucket in 100 to 600 fathoms and is often brought in by halibut fishermen.

A deep-water species dredged up by a "Challenger" expedition, *Scleroptilum gracile* is bright orange in color and grows from six inches to a foot in height, with a row of flowerlike polyps along each of the upper half of the stem. Another species dredged up by the "Challenger" is *Anthoptilum grandiflorum*. This species grows over two feet in height and measures one inch in diameter and has many hundreds of polyps.

Members of the genus *Funiculina* have a short stalk and a more or less rectangular rachis. A representative species is *Funiculina armata* which is a much-branched colony with a horny axis and long clavate, spinose calicles. It grows up to a length of two feet and bears the autozooids in

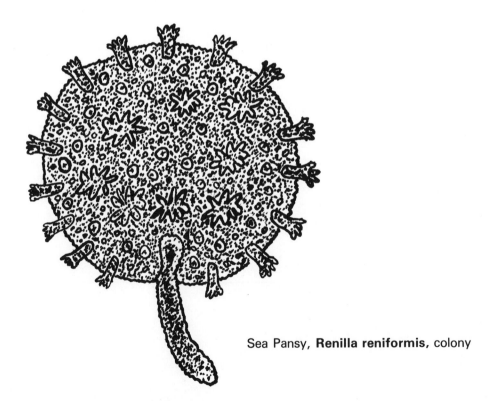

Sea Pansy, **Renilla reniformis**, colony

oblique rows, the siphonozooids being confined to the lower side of the rachis. The autozooids are a deep purple, the rachis yellowish below and brownish above. It is found from Newfoundland to Nantucket in 100 to 400 fathoms.

A remarkable species which has a generally flowerlike appearance is *Renilla reniformis*, popularly known as the Sea Pansy. The rachis is broad and circular or kidney-shaped, with the polyps only on the front or upper surface. There is no axial skeleton and the stalk is soft. The rachis is rose pink or violet in color and the polyps are white. The Sea Pansy is found along the coast of Carolina in shallow water and in the West Indies. A related species, *Renilla amethystina*, occurs in shallow water off southern California. In this species the rachis is violet or amethyst in color, the polyps white.

20. The Zoantharians

The zoantharians are anthozoans with many tentacles and many mesenteries. Most of them secrete a stony or hornlike skeleton and they are frequently of large size. They include the true corals and the sea anemones.

The polyps of these animals are cylindrical in shape and are very contractile. The upper end of the body is the oral disc with a slit-like opening in the center and a siphonoglyph at each end. Radiating series of hollow tentacles surround the mouth. They may be arranged either in one circlet around the edge of the disc or in several or many circlets completely covering the top. They may be in radiating rows or there may be two single circlets, one, called the oral circlet, being close around the mouth, the other, called the marginal circlet, being around the outer edge of the disc.

The internal body cavity is divided into radiating chambers that are separated by thin partitions called septa or mesenteries. Water passes from one chamber to another through pores (ostia) in the mesenteries, and all are open below the gullet or pharnyx into which the mouth opens. The mesenteries are arranged in pairs of different sizes, of which the longest are six in number. These divide the cavity into the radial chambers and are called the primary mesenteries. They are the first to appear in the development of the polyp. Muscle bands extend from the top to the bottom of each mesentery. In the spaces between the primary mesenteries, smaller mesenteries project from the body wall into the chambers, but they do not reach the gullet. They are called the secondary septa or mesenteries. Between the primary and secondary mesenteries are still shorter mesenteries called the tertiary mesenteries. The free edges of the mesenteries below the gullet are expanded into thickened structures called the mesenterial or digestive filaments, which are often much convoluted. They are equipped with glandular cells that secrete digestive juices (enzymes) and with stinging cells (nematocysts). The gonads are near the edge of the mesenteries. There are about 4,000 species of zoantharians.

21. The Antipatharians

The antipatharians are colonial zoantharians that look like the alcyonarians. They have a black, hornlike, and branched central axis with a thin coenenchyma in which there are no spicules embedded. The polyps have six tentacles and six mesenteries. There are about 150 species, known as the black corals. Most of them live in deep seas.

A representative species is *Antipathes larix*. The colony grows up to three feet or more high and is composed of a few long main stalks each with six longitudinal rows of parallel branches from an inch and a half to four inches long. It occurs in the West Indies and in the Mediterranean.

The species *Cirripathes spiralis*, found in the West Indies, the Mediterranean, and the Indian Ocean, is not branched but consists instead of a long, flexible, spiral stalk three or more feet long.

22. The Cerianthideans

The cerianthideans are not true sea anemones but solitary, tube-building anthozoans resembling the anemone, with smooth, muscular, often tapering cylindrical bodies having a terminal pore. They are usually found buried in sand or mud with only the oral disc and two circlets of tentacles protruding, one being an outer, marginal row and the other an inner row around the oral disc. The tentacles are simple, slender, and tapering. There is but one siphonoglyph and the pharnyx is slitlike. The body cavity is divided into as many chambers as there are tentacles in each row, one tentacle of each row opening into each chamber. The mesenteries, which are indefinite in number, are not paired as in the true sea anemones, but merely correspond to similar mesenteries on the opposite side of the body cavity. The retractor and sphincter muscles are weak or altogether lacking in the adults, the ectodermal muscles functioning as retractors. The ectoderm is provided with numerous gland and nettle cells which discharge enough mucus and stinging cells to form a long tube in which the animals live. There are about fifty species.

The species *Cerianthus borealis* is typical of this group. The length of the body is usually seven to nine inches and the width two inches, the expanded tentacles measuring five to six inches across, but it may occasionally measure eighteen inches long and seven inches across the expanded tentacles. The body varies in form according to how it is contracted, and thus may either be tapered towards the end or swollen and urn-shaped. There may be from 150 to 200 marginal tentacles, the oral

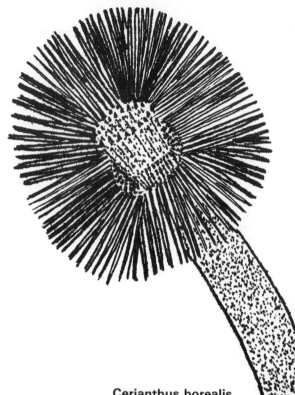

Cerianthus borealis

tentacles being about one-third as long. The body varies in color from a dark chestnut-brown tinged with bluish or purplish, to an orange-brown or greenish-gray; the disc is a pale yellow-brown, deeper around the mouth with fine radiating lines. The tube in which the animal lives is often two feet long and rather smooth inside, and is made of mud and various other materials cemented together by hardened mucus. *Cerianthus borealis* is rather abundant from the Bay of Fundy to Long Island Sound, and occurs in from seven to over 200 fathoms.

A related species, *Cerianthus americanus*, is brown in color with 125 or more tentacles in each of the two circlets, and when fully extended may measure up to two feet in length. It is found in shallow water from Cape Cod to Florida.

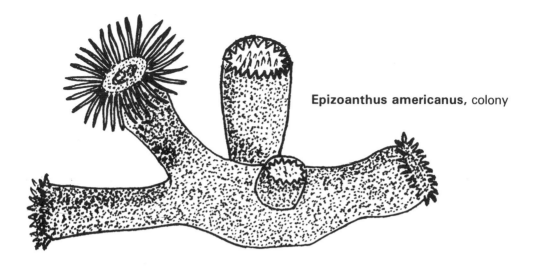

Epizoanthus americanus, colony

23. The Zoanthideans

The zoanthideans are sea anemones that usually grow in colonies from an incrusting or stolon-like base. Many of them grow on hermit crabs, sponges, and hydroids, or even stones on the sea bottom. There are many tentacles in one or two rows, one siphonoglyph, and mesenteries with a characteristic arrangement.

Epizoanthus americanus is a representative species. The colony consists of several individuals rising from a membrane-like base that is commonly attached to stones or to hermit crabs in twenty to 400 fathoms. The anemone's body is more or less encrusted with sand grains and other foreign bodies. The polyps are about an inch in height, with thirty-eight or more tentacles. Quite frequently the membrane-like base has completely absorbed the shell of the crab to which it is attached, so that the crab is covered merely with the membrane-base of the anemone. This species occurs from New Jersey to the Gulf of St. Lawrence.

143

24. The Edwardsiideans

The edwardsiideans are small, slender, solitary sea anemones that usually burrow in the sand with only the oral disc protruding and with a foot tapering or pointed for burrowing. They have from fourteen to forty-eight tentacles and eight fully formed mesenteries, others being rudimentary. There are eight longitudinal ridges, corresponding to the eight mesenteries, on the outer surface which is often encrusted with sand and other foreign substances. There are about twenty species.

A beautiful and delicate species is *Edwardsia elegans*. It measures from three to six inches in length and is about an inch in diameter. There are sixteen tentacles, which vary from yellowish to pale flesh-color with a reddish or orange-red median stripe on the outer surface, extending to near the tip. There is a white or pale yellow spot near the base of the tentacles and also an oval yellow spot with a V-shaped marking on the outer side of the base. The disc is somewhat cone-shaped and striped with eight lines of reddish or purplish-brown, square white spots often occurring between the lines. Beneath the base of the tentacles there is a series of lemon yellow spots that extend around the body and also a band of eight oval, pale yellow spots, each of which is divided by pale orange stripes. This species occurs under stones in shallow water north of Cape Cod.

A common species that occurs from Vineyard Sound southwards,

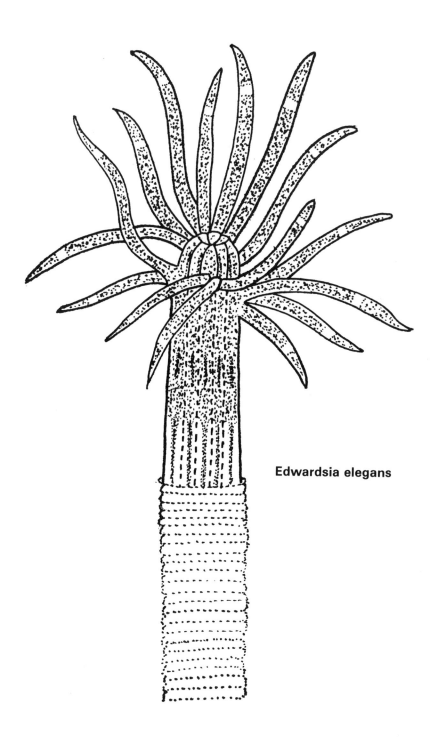

Edwardsia elegans

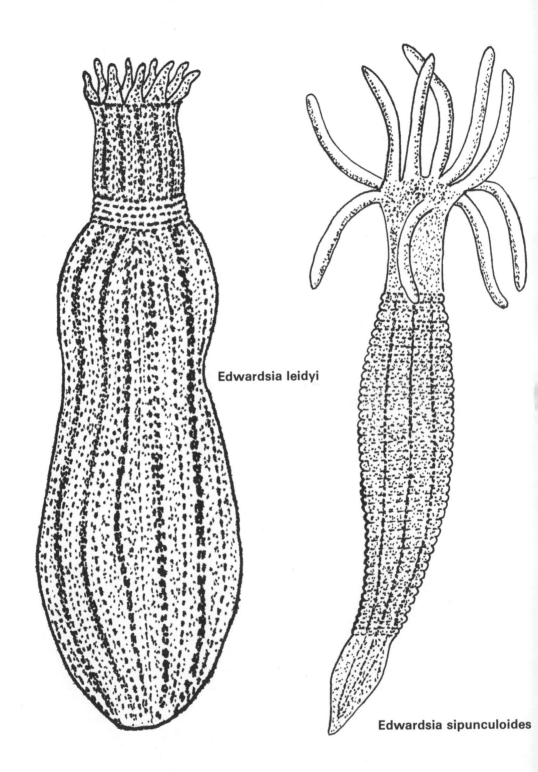

Edwardsia leidyi

Edwardsia sipunculoides

146

Edwardsia leidyi also has sixteen tentacles and is an inch and a quarter long. It is somewhat peculiar in that it is a parasite of the ctenophore or comb jelly, *Mnemiopsis leidyi*.

Unlike the two preceding species, the sea anemone *Edwardsia lineata* has from eighteen to thirty tentacles; it is from an inch to an inch and a quarter long, is cylindrical in form and brown in color. It occurs from Vineyard Sound southwards and is common among worm tubes, rocks, and the like. Another brown species is *Edwardsia sipunculoides*, which has twenty to thirty-six tentacles and when extended measures almost five inches in length. It occurs in shallow water from Cape Cod northwards.

25. The Actiniarians

The actiniarians are the true sea anemones, probably the best known animals of the ocean margin. They may most often be found in tide-pools at low water and in submerged places in the crevices of rocks. Anyone who is in the habit of exploring along the seashore is familiar with their flowerlike appearance, whence their name.

The sea anemones are usually solitary animals, of large size, and are often brightly colored. They occur in all parts of the world and at all depths, and usually attach themselves temporarily to some more or less stationary object by their broad sucker-like foot, though they can move about slowly. Some of them live in the sand and a few are free-swimming. There are about a thousand species of these curious and, at times, beautiful animals.

The sea anemone's body consists of an oral disc, a column, and a base. It is cylindrical in form, soft and contractile, and lacks a skeleton. The oral disc is flat, circular, and sometimes has a lobed margin. The tentacles are simple, hollow, and taper to a point or to a ball-like enlargement provided with batteries of nematocysts. The tentacles may be few or many, and may be arranged in two or many circles or in radiating rows, though when numerous they seem to be without any definite arrangement. In some species they cover the greater part of the oral disc.

The cylindrical body is known as the column, which is partly separated from the base by a constriction, the base itself often being expanded into a circular pedal disc, which can adhere to various objects on the sea bottom or wrap itself around shells or stones, or flatten out on the side of a rock. The anemone is able to travel slowly from place to place by extending parts of its pedal disc. The mouth, though occasionally round, is usually slitlike and in the center of a clear, smooth zone which separates it from the tentacles. The food is taken in through the mouth, is digested in the gastrovascular cavity, and then passes through all the chambers of the cavity as nutritive fluid, the undigested particles being expelled through the mouth again. The mesenteries, which divide the internal cavity into chambers, are arranged in definite radiating patterns, usually in pairs with the muscle-bands facing each other, except in the case of the mesenteries on either side of the siphonoglyphs which have the muscle-bands facing outwards. The anemone is sensitive to various stimuli and at the least alarm can contract its body by means of the longitudinal muscles, as well as those that are arranged around the circumference of the body, changing from a beautiful flowerlike form into a shapeless, unattractive, inconspicuous mass.

The gonads and mesenterial filaments are located on the free edges of the mesenteries. The eggs when mature pass into the gastrovascular cavity where they are fertilized by the sperms, after which they pass out through the mouth as free-swimming planulae to eventually settle down on the sea bottom and develop into adult polyps. The sea anemones may also reproduce asexually by splitting in half or by budding smaller individuals from the side of the parent.

Sea anemones vary greatly in form and color and when expanded suggest flowers, though not the ones for which they are named, resembling more closely chrysanthemums or dahlias. They occur on every shore, the larger and more highly colored species in tropical waters. Many species are littoral and are found in tide-pools of rocky caverns, on the under side of rocks, and on the piles of wharves and bridges at low-water mark. They are among the most beautiful and conspicuous inhabitants of the tide-pools along the seacoast where, when fully expanded, they form a sea garden filled with flowerlike crowns of various colors. But they are anything but flowerlike, rather more often death traps for the small organisms that come within reach of the tentacles. Sea anemones are not only carnivorous but also voracious, and feed on all kinds of small animals which they capture and kill with their tentacles and stinging cells. An anemone that lives on the Great Barrier Reef of Australia and measures two feet across is, strangely enough, inhabited by small red and

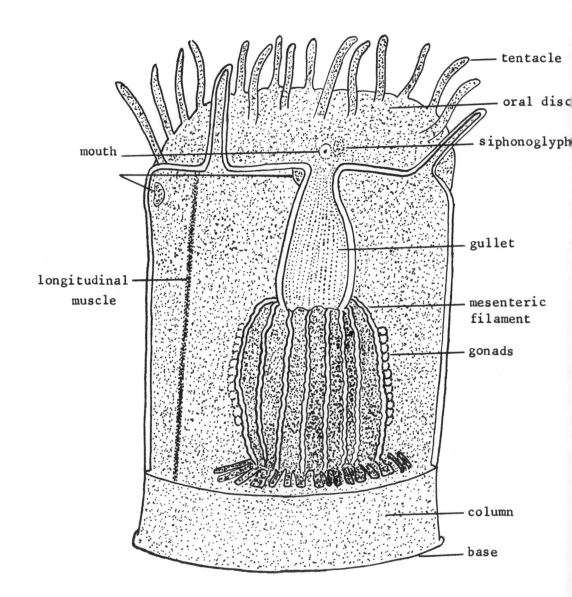

tentacle

oral disc

siphonoglyph

mouth

gullet

longitudinal muscle

mesenteric filament

gonads

column

base

Longitudinal section of a typical actinian or sea anemone

150

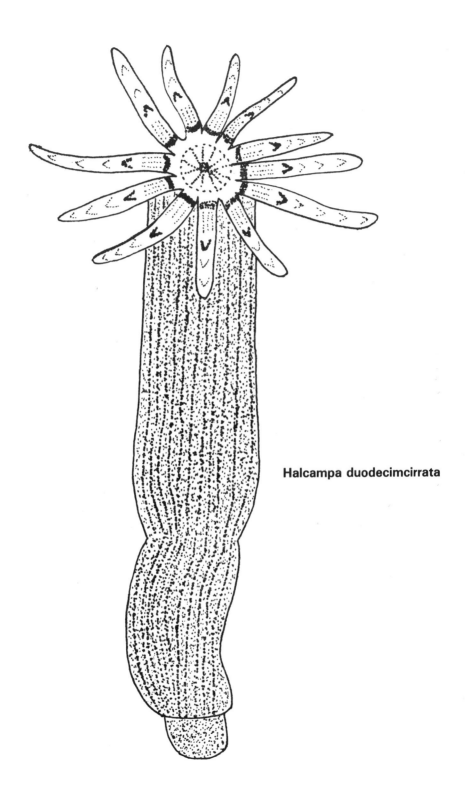

Halcampa duodecimcirrata

white fish that swim in and out through the mouth without in any way being injured by the tentacles or stinging cells.

Halcampa duodecimcirrata is a species that occupies crevices in the sea bottom and among rocks, though it is able to move about. It has a long and slender body with longitudinal grooves and lacks a pedal disc, the lower end being rounded or pointed and sometimes swollen. The tentacles are short and twelve in number and there are few mesenteries. The column is very changeable in form and is usually covered with sand. There is a concentric circle of purplish-brown near the base of the tentacles. On either side of each tentacle there is a spot of reddish-brown near the base and six crescent-shaped transverse spots of reddish-brown alternating with flesh-color. The body or column is salmon-color with purplish-brown spots. This species occurs along the coast of Maine to the Bay of Fundy.

A species common in the summer from Cape Cod to Nova Scotia, *Siphonactinia parasiticum*, has a mouth that is prolonged into a three-lobed proboscis and is parasitic on jellyfish to which it becomes attached by means of the mouth lobes. The body, which varies in color from flesh-color to light brown or greenish-brown, is soft, naked, and extremely changeable in form. When fully extended it may be as much as three and a half inches long, but when contracted it may assume an elliptical or ovate shape. There are usually twelve tentacles. They are about one-half inch long, taper from a swollen base, and have a pore at the end. There are six pairs of mesenteries and twelve grooves, corresponding to the mesenteries. A pedal disc is lacking but instead there is a central contractile pore. Although parasitic in habit, the species is often found in sand.

Whitish or salmon-color, the anemone *Eloactus producta* lives buried in the sand or on the under side of stones in shallow water from South Carolina to Cape Cod. It has a slender, very contractile body, with a diameter of about three-quarters of an inch, and when fully extended may be almost ten inches long. There are twenty tentacles in two rows, which are short and blunt or with a knob at the ends, and as many longitudinal ridges.

Found off the coast of Southern California where it burrows in sand and mud, *Harenactis attenuata* is dirty white in color with a body of not quite an inch long and a diameter of about three-quarters of an inch. It has twenty-four tentacles in one series.

Occurring in shallow water north of Cape Cod, colonies of *Bunodes stella* are often found in large numbers in the crevices of ridges covered

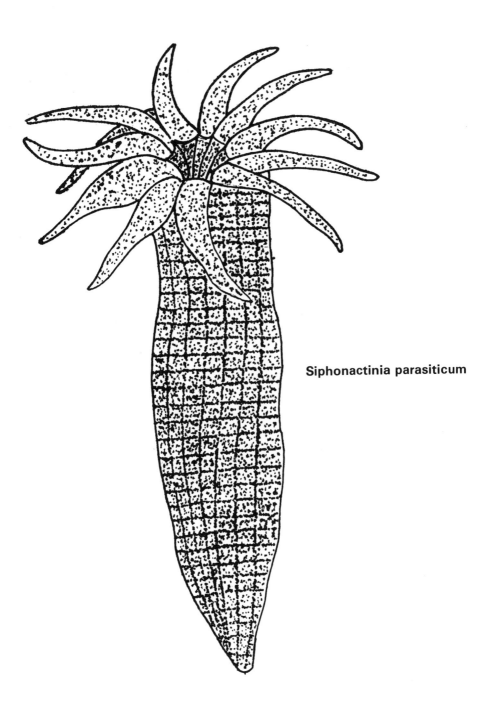

Siphonactinia parasiticum

153

with algae, especially in sheltered tide-pools. Sometimes this sea anemone lies buried in the sand with only its tentacles exposed. Occasionally it may be found under stones. The body, which is a translucent olive-green, varying to flesh-color and to a dark green, is about two inches high, the outer surface covered with longitudinal rows of tubercles.

The characteristic feature of the sea anemone *Epiactis prolifera*, is the band of egg pits, which may number from thirty to forty, that surrounds the outer surface of the body just below its middle. The body is not quite half an inch in height and about the same in diameter, and there are about ninety-six tentacles. The species occurs along the Pacific coast from

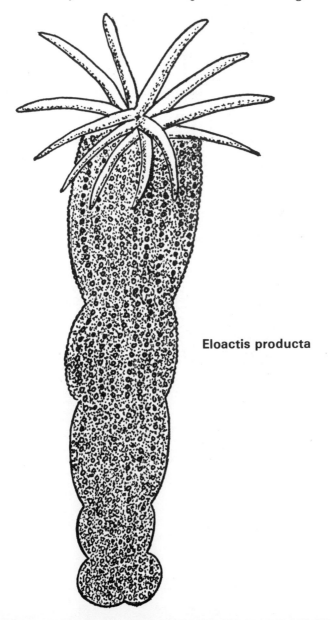

Eloactis producta

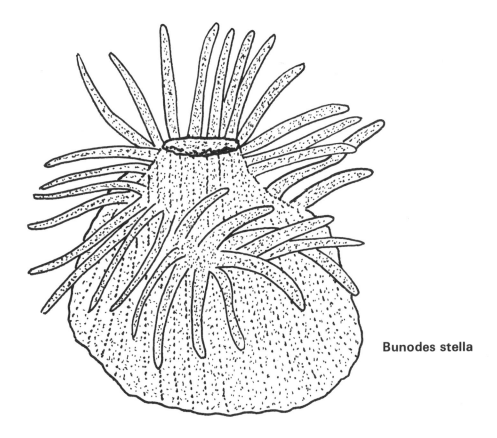

Bunodes stella

Puget Sound to San Francisco.

A very large, stout, and brightly colored species, *Tealia crassicornis*, is commonly called the Thick-petaled Rose-anemone from its large, thick tentacles and the color of its body. Its color varies, however, often being bluish-green mottled with crimson, sometimes bright cherry-red, the tentacles somewhat lighter in shade or flesh-colored. It attains a height of about two inches and a diameter of not quite five inches. The column, which is soft, flexible, and very changeable in form, has on its outer surface many scattered tubercles or suckers and is more or less covered with sand, bits of shell, etc. There are 160 tentacles. The animal is found in shallow water in northern seas, extending southward to Puget Sound and Cape Cod and along the coast of Europe.

The sea anemone *Bolocera tuediae*, may easily be recognized by its large, cylindrical orange or red body and its very large, non-retractile tentacles, the latter being easily discarded. The body is two to three inches in diameter and the diameter across the tentacles frequently reaches six to eight inches. The column is orange-red in color as are the disc and tentacles. The numerous thick folds around the margin of the

155

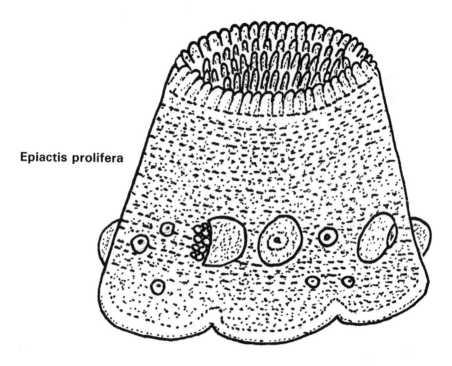

Epiactis prolifera

mouth are a bright red and the two siphonoglyphs are also bright red or rose-color varying to purple. This species occurs from the Bay of Fundy and the outer side of Nova Scotia, south to Cape Cod and Martha's Vineyard.

The anemone *Bolocera multicornis* is also a large red species. The column is very short and thick and there are more than 200 tentacles which, when expanded, give the animal the appearance of being a red hemisphere covered with moving tentacles.

The species *Paractis rapiformis* is usually found buried in the sand near low-water mark from Cape Cod to Hatteras. The body is about three inches in height and about an inch in diameter and is covered with fine longitudinal grooves. The mouth is surrounded by a circle of short, cylindrical tentacles, all of the same length. The surface of the body is pinkish and there is a small pedal disc. A related species, *Paractis perdix* is remarkable for its many tentacles which may number as many as 400 and which crown the entire top of the column, the latter reaching a height of three or four inches with a broad oral disc as much as five inches in diameter.

Actinostola callosa is a massive species, having a height of six to seven inches and an oral disc eight to ten inches in diameter. The many tentacles are arranged in four rows around the outer edge of the oral disc,

The Thick-petaled Rose-anemone, **Tealia crassicornis**

Bolocera tuediae

the inner tentacles much longer than the outer. This anemone is found off the New England coast in forty-five to 300 fathoms.

A yellowish or pale flesh-colored anemone, *Sagartia modesta* is usually found at about low-tide mark where it burrows in the sand and at times is difficult to find because its coloration blends with its environment. The body is cylindrical, about two and a half inches high with a diameter of about five-eighths of an inch, and is provided with a strong pedal disc. There are sixty or more tentacles which are delicate in texture, slender and tapering, and gray in color, verging on green. The species occurs in Long Island and Vineyard sounds.

Sagartia luciae is a handsome species, olive-green in color with about twelve longitudinal orange or yellow stripes. It is between half and three-quarters of an inch in height. There are from twenty-five to fifty long, delicate tentacles, pale green in color tinged with white. This anemone is very common on stones and shells in tide pools and occurs from Florida to Massachusetts and along the Pacific coast.

Common under stones and in the sand in shallow water from Cape Cod to North Carolina, *Sagartia leucolena*, popularly known as the White-armed Anemone, is a small and delicate species. It has an elongated, cylindrical body which, when extended, may measure an inch and a half in height, and which may be covered with tiny papillae. It is also very translucent so that the edges of the mesenteries may be seen through its sides. The color varies from a delicate flesh to white. There are forty or more tentacles which are very slender, tapering to the tip, and white, whence the popular name of the animal. The species is quite sensitive to light and therefore tends to seek dark corners among the rocks.

One of the most conspicuous and abundant of the sea anemones along our coast is the species *Metridium dianthus*, popularly known as the Brown Anemone. It is world-wide in distribution and ranges from around the Arctic region southward along both our coasts and along the coast of Europe. It is found near low-water mark, in tide-pools, on the underside of large stones, in sheltered crevices of rocks, and on the piles of wharves and bridges. It has a velvety smooth column, up to four inches in height and three inches broad, the column being crowned with a widely expanded disc which is divided into waved lobes and covered with numerous small and slender tentacles that appear like a fringe that covers the upper side of the disc halfway to the oval mouth. Large individuals may have as many as a thousand tentacles, with a corresponding number of pairs of mesenteries. The color of the animal is exceedingly variable. Though the column is commonly yellowish-brown it may also be pink, white, salmon, orange, or dark brown, or striped or mottled with

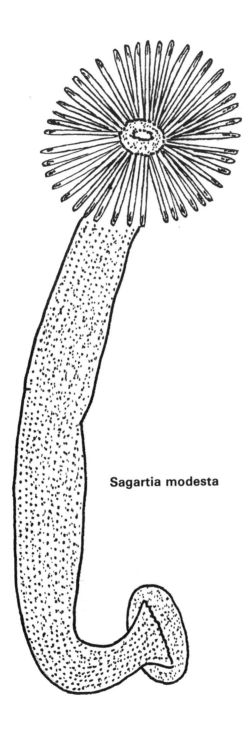

Sagartia modesta

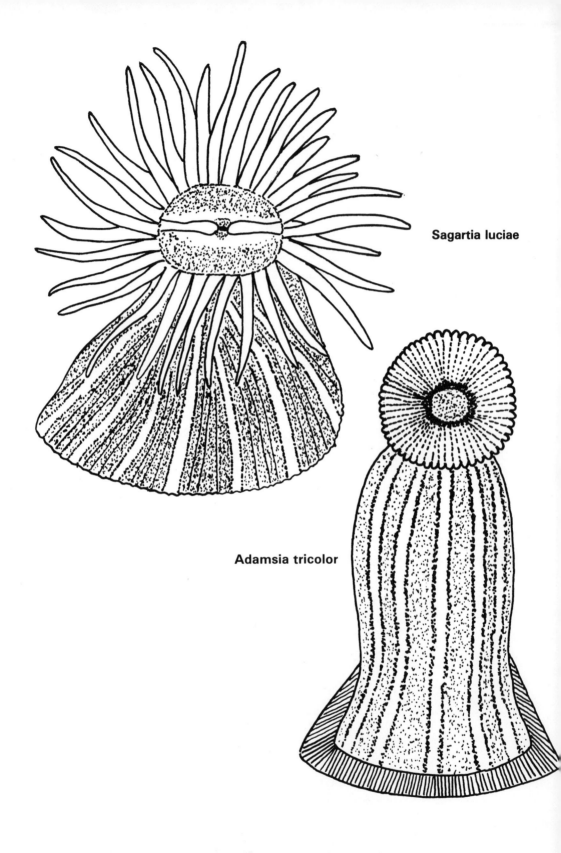

Sagartia luciae

Adamsia tricolor

different colors. The disc is lighter or flesh-color and the tentacles vary though they are usually grayish with tips of brighter colors. When irritated the animal throws out numbers of acontia which protect it from the attacks of its many enemies.

A strongly expanded pedal disc is a characteristic feature of the anemone *Adamsia tricolor*. This species may be three inches in height and nearly two inches in diameter, and has numerous tentacles, large individuals with as many as five hundred. The animal usually attaches itself to the shells of hermit crabs and may be found in shallow water from North Carolina to Florida.

In the species *Actinauge rugosa*, the cylindrical column has an expanded base which is conspicuous as a thin rim running completely around it. The column is, moreover, rather peculiar in having a thick and almost rigid cortex. In the upper part of the column there is a transverse row of a dozen or more compressed tubercles which look like small horizontal shelves. The upper edge of the column is also irregularly scalloped and the entire column has a tendency to be wrinkled. There are ninety-six or more stout tentacles. The species occurs in fifty to one hundred fathoms along the New England coast to Nova Scotia.

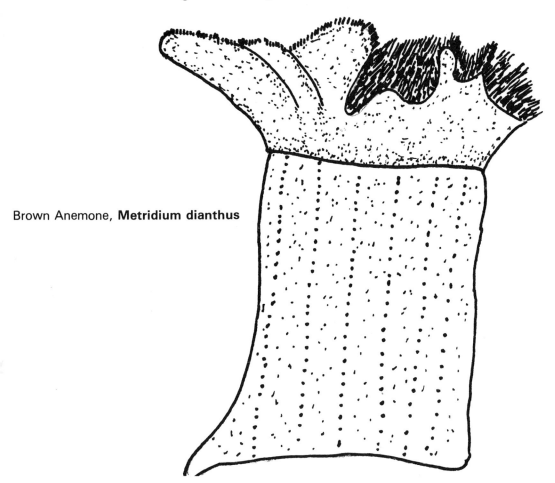

Brown Anemone, **Metridium dianthus**

26. The Madreporarians

The madreporarians are the stony corals. They are the animals that build the coral reefs and coral islands. The coral polyps resemble the sea anemones and are arranged on the same principle, that is, on the radial plan. Like them, they may be either solitary or colonial. But they differ from the sea anemones in that they are able to secrete from the basal ectoderm a very hard skeleton of calcium carbonate. This is built up beneath and around the base of the body, usually in the form of a cup (calyx or corallite) in which the polyp or zooid can retract itself. The skeleton consists essentially of a system of radiating vertical plates or septa. These project into the interior of the polyp, but are always covered with the three layers of the body wall and alternate in a general way with the mesenteries. As a rule the outer edges of the septa connect with an outer wall called the theca, which is the outer part of the cup in which the polyp sits. There is often a central column (columella) in the middle of the cup. As the polyps grow they build up the theca and the septa, gradually withdrawing from the deeper portions, which may become cut off by horizontal partitions called the tabulae.

The polyps reproduce by budding and by self-division. The way in which the budding or fission takes place determines the shape of the colony, which may take a variety of forms. If the budding is confined to certain individuals of the colony, as occurs in some species, branched forms result. In instances where fission occurs, hemispherical masses are formed which are sometimes perfectly symmetrical. In the genus *Astraea* the polyps are enclosed separately, but in the genus *Meandrina* fission is confined to the upper half of the polyps, with the result that a complex polyp is formed, with several mouths opening into a common gastrovascular cavity, thus making long serpentine furrows on the colony.

The stony corals live in shallow water, 300 feet being the maximum depth at which they are found, and most of them occur in tropical or subtropical waters. A few, however, occur in temperate and even in Arctic seas. There are over 2500 species.

The species *Oculina diffusa*, popularly known as the Eyed Coral, is a treelike, very much branched coral, the branches forming an angle of about thirty degrees. The corallites or cups, about an eighth of an inch in diameter, are arranged spirally on the branches, and are more or less widely separated from one another. It is often common in shallow water from North Carolina to Florida.

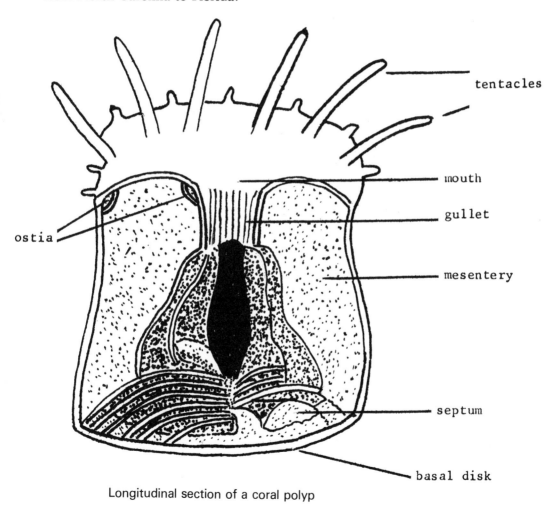

Longitudinal section of a coral polyp

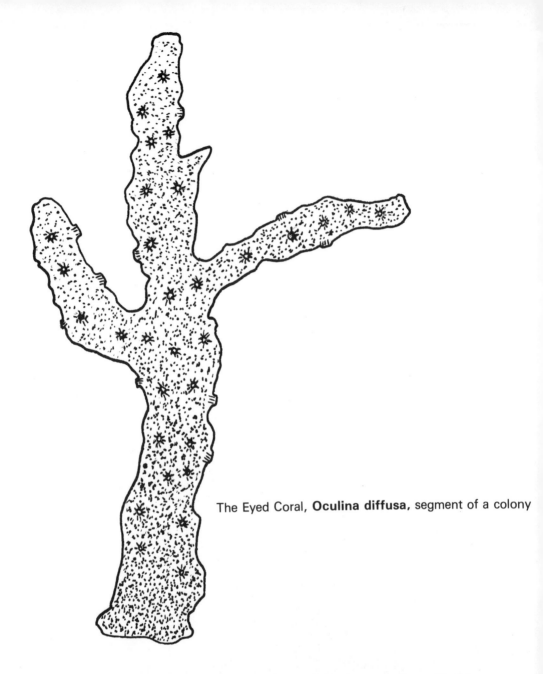

The Eyed Coral, **Oculina diffusa,** segment of a colony

The principal coral found along the Atlantic coast from Florida to Cape Cod is the Star Coral, *Astrangia danae*, a beautiful little coral growing in patches on stones, shells, etc., in shallow water. It is a small colony with from five to thirty individuals, the colony about four inches in diameter and two inches high. The polyps, not more than a quarter of an inch in height, are whitish or slightly pinkish in color and are so trans-

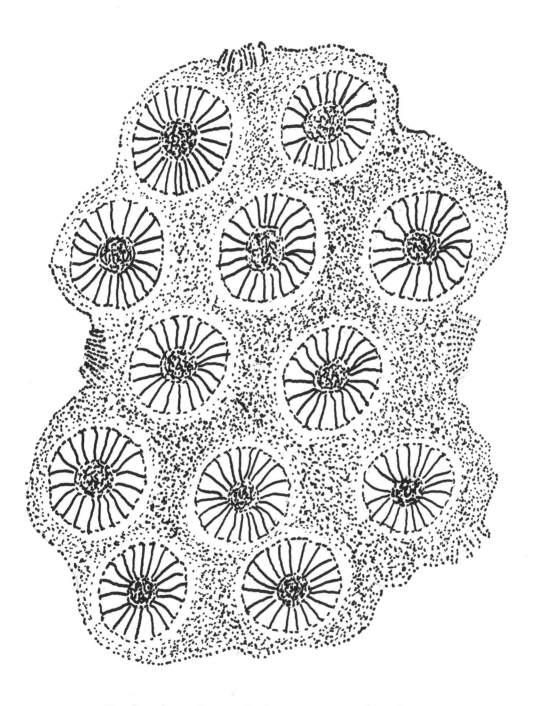

The Star Coral, **Astrangia danae**, segment of a colony

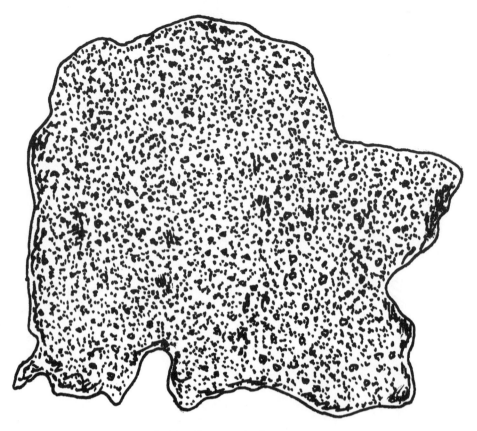

Orbicella annularis

parent that the edges of the mesenteries show through the polyp wall as little vertical white lines. The little polyps, looking like tiny stars, are conspicuous as they lie imbedded in the stony material. A related species, *Astrangia insignifica*, with orange or coral-red polyps, occurs in the littoral zone from Point Conception southwards to Baja California.

The species *Orbicella annularis* is a rather massive coral, somewhat globular in outline with the zooids distinct and separated by deep concave spaces. It is found off the coast of Florida and in the West Indies.

A colony from an inch and a half to more than three inches long and half as broad, *Meandrina meandrites* has a single large main groove and large septa. The zooids are confluent and the tentacles, mesenteries, and septae are arranged in rows. It also occurs in the West Indies and off the coast of Florida. A related species, *Meandrina sinuosa*, is commonly known as the Brain Coral. It is an incrusting and massive colony, ten inches or more in diameter and hemispherical in shape, the surface with numerous sinuous ridges, which are the septa, and grooves. Its shape, together with the peculiar serpentine corallites, makes it look very much like the human brain and hence its name is quite appropriate. The polyps are bright yellow. It is found in the same range as the preceding.

The species *Acropora cervicornis* is the well-known Staghorn Coral. It is a branching species that attains large size, as much as three feet or more long and twenty inches wide, its branches reminiscent of those of the stag, hence its name. The coral is porous and contains canals that connect the polyps which are rather small and crowded. The cups are small and deep and without a columella. The terminal polyps have six, the lateral polyps have twelve tentacles. The staghorn coral occurs in the West Indies and off the coast of Florida. A related species, *Acropora palmata*, found in the same range, is similar except that the branches have become fused together forming large fan-shaped masses.

Known as the Mushroom Coral, *Fungia elegans* is a solitary species, round and thick, and about two and a half inches in diameter, the upper side convex, the lower side concave. The living disc covers the septa with numerous tentacles rising from its surface. The embryo develops into a conical coral called a trophozooid, the upper part of which expands,

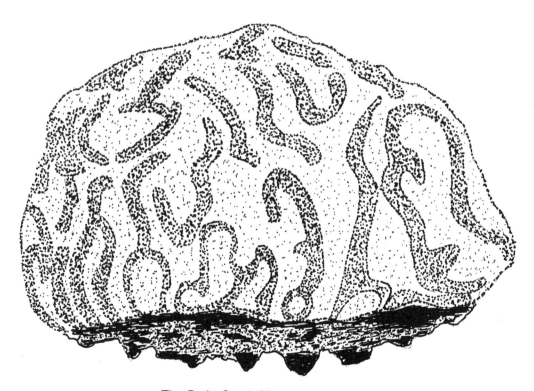

The Brain Coral, **Meandrina sinuosa**

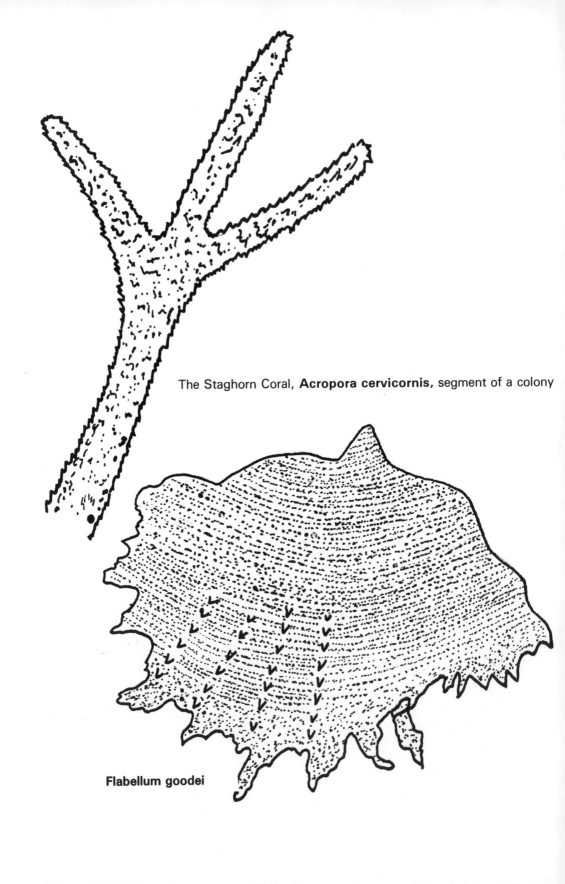

The Staghorn Coral, **Acropora cervicornis,** segment of a colony

Flabellum goodei

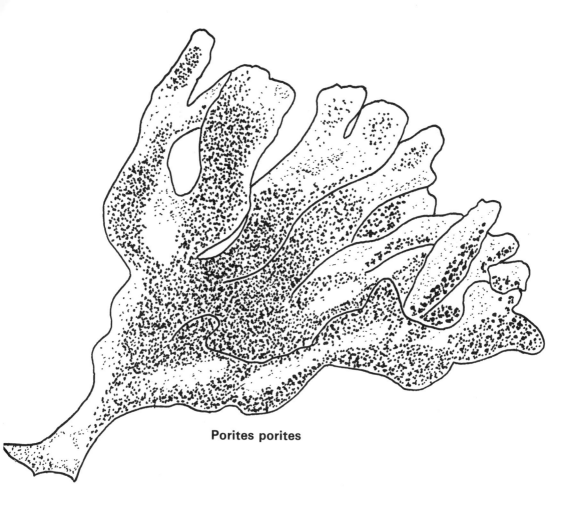

Porites porites

breaks off, and becomes the adult coral, a process which may repeat itself a number of times. The species is found in the Gulf of California.

The species *Flabellum goodei* is a solitary coral which is more or less flattened or fan-shaped and tapers to the base which is somewhat pointed. The base is imbedded in the sea bottom when the animal is young but may become detached later. The height of the coral may reach three inches and the diameter may be as much as five inches. When living the coral is salmon color with brown stripes. It is a very fragile species and is found from Newfoundland to Florida in 200 to 500 fathoms. Another species of the same genus, *Flabellum angulare*, is similar, except that the cup is five-sided in shape and beautifully symmetrical, with the septa forming a radiating pattern in the interior of the shallow cup.

Porites porites is another porous species, the colony more or less branching. The zooids are small and close together, the cups with about twelve short septa. A columella is present but frequently indistinct. The species occurs in the West Indies and off the coast of Florida. It sometimes forms very large colonies.

27. Coral Reefs and Coral Islands

Coral reefs and coral islands have been built and are being built by count-less coral animals, more specifically by the epidermal cells of the polyps, each one secreting its cup-shaped skeleton. The polyps live for a while and then die, new generations secreting new calcareous cups upon the old ones. Only the surface of a coral mass is alive. And a living coral is quite different in appearance from the bleached skeletons commonly seen.

The coral polyps build various types of reefs, atolls, and islands, principally in tropical seas where the temperature of the water is at least 60° F. Two major regions where coral reefs and islands occur are the Caribbean area, including Florida, Bermuda, the Bahamas and the West Indies, and the Indo-Pacific area, known as the Coral Sea, extending from Australia to Hawaii and the Philippines. The best known coral islands are the Maldives of the Indian Ocean, Wake Island, the Marshalls, and the Fiji Islands of the Pacific, and those located in the Bahama Islands region—for instance Bermuda, whose houses are built from coral block mined from certain areas. The Mariana Islands, of historic interest, are also coral.

Three types of coral reef formation may be distinguished: fringing reef, barrier reef, and atoll reef. A fringing reef is a ridge of coral that has been built up from the sea bottom and so near to land that there is no navigable channel between it and the shore.

170

A barrier reef is one that is separated from the shore by a wide deep channel which may provide passage for fairly large ships. Such a reef, however, may constitute a menace to shipping. The largest and most famous of the barrier reefs is the Great Barrier Reef of Australia which is like a giant breakwater stretching for some 1300 miles along the northeastern coast of the continent. At some points the reef is more than a hundred miles from the Australian mainland; at other points it is no more than ten miles from the coast. The channel is from sixty to 150 feet deep. The outer, or eastern side, of the reef forms a mighty rampart all the way to the ocean floor, which is some 500 feet below, and against which the Pacific Ocean pounds in all its fury.

The Great Barrier Reef is not a single or continuous reef but a complex system of individual reefs, islands, channels, and shoals. When the tide is low great expanses of bare coral formation are revealed, which provide a rich display of marine life. Each and every tide-pool is replete with a seemingly endless variety of marine animals: reef fishes, starfishes, many different kinds of corals, and the giant clams for which the reef is famous, some of which weigh a quarter of a ton. Also among its inhabitants is a little cone-shell snail whose venomous tongue can kill a man, and the notorious stonefish, probably the deadliest and certainly the ugliest fish in the sea. But despite such dangers, the reef is a showcase for many of the living wonders to be found in the sea.

An atoll is made up of one or two islands consisting of a belt of coral reef surrounding a central lagoon. Many atolls in the mid-Pacific have lagoons varying from a few hundred yards to many miles in diameter. The atoll of Bikini, for instance, has a lagoon area of 280 square miles and a land area of only 2.87 square miles. Wake Island and Tarawa are atolls famous for the part they played in World War II. The horseshoe atoll of western Texas, a prolific source of petroleum, now lies buried under thousands of feet of rocks but existed as an atoll in the shallow seas that covered the area millions of years ago.

The coral reef is a veritable jungle of sea animals. Reef fish, turtles, crabs, conches, barracudas, sharks, and the evil-looking moray eels are among the inhabitants of a reef, animals that live and breed within the tropical coral community. Mollusks, worms, crabs, starfishes, and sea urchins also find a home there, though they are ungrateful creatures that bore into and penetrate the reef in various ways and by so doing eventually destroy it. Large fragments are detached by their depredations and are either carried by the waves to distant places or are ground to sand which fill the crevices of the reef and adds to its solidity.

The secret of a coral's existence is due in large measure to the microscopic plant cells that live within its tissues, in a sort of mutual

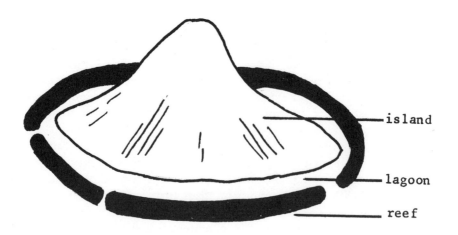

island

lagoon

reef

Fringing reef

island

lagoon

reef

Barrier reef

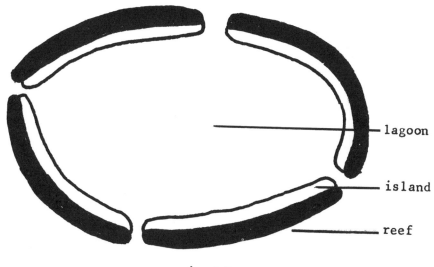

lagoon

island

reef

An atoll

partnership. As long as there is sufficient light—and this is the reason why corals are not found at a depth of much more than 100 feet, for at that depth the intensity of light is too weak to support photosynthesis— the plant cells grow and multiply, nourished in part by the carbon dioxide and nutrient salts furnished by the animal. In return they provide the coral animal with oxygen, which is a by-product of photosynthesis, and any excess carbohydrates manufactured by the plants in addition to those they need themselves. Without the plants the coral animal world suffocate in the congested masses of the reef. Of course, the coral animals cannot exist solely on the nutrients that the plants provide; they must also secure other food in the form of small organisms that they capture in the manner of other coelenterates.

The reef corals are able to survive the loss of the plant cells for a time, and occasionally they have to do so, as in the Caribbean where hurricanes occur annually. The heavy rains that accompany a hurricane sometimes so dilute the sea water that bathes the corals that some plant cells are killed. If the dilution is so severe that many plant cells die, many corals will die also, especially those found within a few feet of the sea surface. However, most corals survive and before long have regained a fresh supply of plant cells.

28. The Origin of the Coelenterates

It is rather idle to speculate on the origin of the coelenterates since our present knowledge of how these animals developed is somewhat limited. But it appears that they probably arose from a two-layered animal, perhaps akin to a free-swimming ciliated form like the planula of certain hydroids. According to present hypothesis, this two-layered form became modified into a gastrula form (a cup or open-mouthed sac with walls composed of two layers of cells) having a body wall consisting of an outer layer of cells, the ectoderm, and an inner layer, the endoderm, the ectoderm being protective and sensory in function, the endoderm digestive and absorptive, and between which there appeared a jellylike connective tissue, the mesoglea. This ancestral form had a central cavity, a mouth, a sense organ opposite the mouth, muscle and nerve cells in a primitive stage of differentiation, and tentacles, and looked something like a medusa. It is further supposed that the larvae of these medusa-like ancestors may have become attached to a substratum and then become modified into hydroid polyps.

29. The History of the Coelenterates

The coelenterates were known to the ancients, and the Greek philosopher Aristotle was acquainted with many of them. At his time and through the succeeding ages these exotic animals were considered to be either plants or plant-animals (zoophytes) by the various naturalists who observed and studied them, and who believed them to be the connecting link between the plant and animal kingdoms. The polyps and the corals were generally regarded as plants, the individual animals being the flowers.

Such views remained in force until 1744 when Trembley established the animal nature of hydras and 1753 when Peyssonnel demonstrated the animal nature of corals. Following such discoveries a new era in the study of these animals began, and during the ensuing years many species were described and figured, but for a long time the relation of the polyp to the medusa remained unknown. In 1799 the French zoologist Cuvier undertook to study the anatomy of the medusa and some years later, in 1812, he brought the polyps and medusae together in the single type group known as Animalia-Radiata.

From that time on a great deal more was learned of the anatomy of both the medusa and the polyp, but it was not until the early 1840s that the relation of one to the other was fully explained and the principle of alternation of generations formulated. Then in 1847 the German zoologist Leuckart dissolved the "Radiata" of Cuvier and created the phylum Coelenterata, at the same time calling attention to the fundamental   sac form of the body and the absence of a body cavity. Two years later the English biologist Huxley showed that the walls of the sac were made up of two layers which he called the ectoderm and the endoderm. In 1851 the term Hydromedusa was introduced by Vogt, in 1856 that of Hydrozoa by Huxley, and in 1891 that of Scyphozoa by Claus.

The first important American work on the coelenterates was J. D. Dana's report of the Zoophyta of the Wilkes Expedition in 1846. The Swiss naturalist Louis Agassiz and his son Alexander, together with their pupils and followers, made many valuable contributions to the literature of the coelenterates and did the most to extend our knowledge of American species.

30. The Economic Importance of the Coelenterates

The coelenterates are of some economic importance by virtue of the reefs, atolls, and islands that they build. Several species serve as food in the Orient, and in Italy two species of Anthozoa are eaten under the name of Ogliole. The precious corals, which are usually bright red or pink and which are decoratively carved or otherwise used in jewelry, were at one time the source of a flourishing industry but have recently been supplanted by synthetics. The industry still continues but is much reduced from its previous production.

Glossary

ABORAL	The side of the body opposite the mouth
ACONTIUM, *PL.* ACONTIA	A vibratile thread-like organ provided with stinging cells in certain sea anemones
ACROCYST	A brood-chamber found in certain campanularian hydroids
ACTINULA	A larval form of certain hydroids
ALGAE	Simple green plants
ALTERNATION OF GENERATIONS	The alternate succession of sexual and asexual generations in the life cycle of a plant or animal
ASEXUAL	Reproduction by division or budding and not through the agency of sex cells (sperms and eggs)
ATOLL REEF	A horseshoe or ring-shaped island or islands consisting of a belt of coral reef surrounding a central lagoon
AUTOZOOID	A feeding zooid in the Pennatulacea
BARRIER REEF	A coral reef roughly parallel to the shore but separated from it by a lagoon

BLASTOSTYLE	The reproductive polyp of a campanularian hydroid
BUD	The developing lateral branch of an organism such as the hydra
BUDDING	The production of offspring by the development of a lateral branch from a part of the body
CALICLE	The cavity of a coral containing a polyp
CALYX	Any structure resembling a cup
CELL	A small mass or unit of protoplasm surrounded by a cell membrane and containing one or more nuclei
CERATINE	A hornlike substance forming the skeleton in certain corals
CILIA	Vibratory projections from the free surface of certain cells
CINCLIDES	One of the pores through which the acontia of sea anemones are protruded
CLASS	A main division of a phylum
CNIDOBLAST	A stinging cell containing a nematocyst
CNIDOCIL	A hairlike process projecting from a stinging cell
COENENCHYMA	The soft parts of an alcyonarian colony
COLONY	A group of individuals of the same species which are organically attached
COLUMELLA	The central pillar in the calyx of many corals
COLUMN	The body of a sea anemone as distinguished from the base and disc
CORALLITE	That part of the skeleton of a coral formed by a single polyp
CRENATE	Having the margin cut into rounded projections or scallops
CTENOPHORE	A member of the phylum Ctenophora, a group of marine animals that resemble coelenterate jellyfishes

DACTYLOZOOID	A form of zooid having no mouth, found in certain hydrozoans
DENDRITIC	Arborescent, branching
DIGESTION	The conversion of complex unabsorbable food material into soluble forms that may be absorbed
DIMORPHISM	Difference in color, form, size, structure, etc., between two types of individuals of the same species
ECOSYSTEM	A biotic community together with its non-living environment
ECTODERM	The outermost layer of cells in the Coelenterata
EGG	The non-motile gamete developed by the female
EMBRYO	A young animal which is passing through its development stages, usually within the egg membranes or within the maternal uterus
ENDODERM	The innermost layer of cells in the Coelenterata
ENZYME	A substance produced by living cells that causes specific chemical changes but does not itself undergo significant change
EPHYRA	A youthful stage in the growth of a scyphomedusan
EPIDERMIS	The outer cellular layer or layers covering the external surface of a many-celled animal
EPITHELIAL CELL	A cell of the epithelium
EPITHELIUM	Usually a sheet of cells covering either external or internal surfaces of the body
EXCRETION	The discharge of metabolic wastes
EXUMBRELLA	The aboral side of a medusa
FAMILY	The principal subdivision of an order
FERTILIZATION	The union of a mature sperm and a mature ovum

180

FLAGELLUM *PL.* FLAGELLA	A vibratory thread-like projection of certain cells
FLOAT	In certain pelagic animals, an air sac or other light structure containing air or gas, serving to buoy up the body
FRINGING REEF	A ridge of coral built up from the sea bottom, located so near to land that no navigable channel exists between it and the shore
GAMETE	A sex cell, either the sperm cell or egg cell
GASTROVASCULAR SPACE	The central cavity in the Coelenterata
GASTRODERMIS	An inner cell layer in the hydra
GASTROZOOID	A feeding zooid of a siphonophore colony
GENUS	The taxonomic subdivision of a family
GASTRULA	A stage in the development of the embryo in which two cell layers, ectoderm and endoderm, are present
GONAD	The organ, either testis or ovary, in which the reproductive cells, sperms or ova, are produced
GONANGIUM, *PL.* GONANGIA	The cuticular covering or gonotheca of the blastostyle in campanularian hydroids
GONOPHORE	A reproductive zooid of a hydroid colony
GONOSOME	The medusoid stage of a hydromedusan
GONOTHECA	The cuticular outer covering of the blastostyle
GONOZOOID	The reproductive zooid of a siphonophore colony
HERMAPHRODITIC	An individual having both male and female reproductive organs
HYDRANTH	An individual feeding polyp in a hydroid colony
HYDROCLADIUM, *PL.* HYDROCLADIA	Small branches in the Plumulariidae bearing the polyps
HYDROCAULUS	The stem of a hydroid colony

181

HYDROID	The sessile, asexual generation of the Hydromedusae and Scyphomedusae
HYDRORHIZA	The root-like projection of a hydroid colony by which it is attached
HYDROTHECA	The transparent membrane that extends from the perisarc and surrounds the main part of a hydranth
HYPOSTOME	The projection of a hydroid's body which bears the mouth
INGESTION	The act of taking any substance from the outside, especially food, into the digestive tract of an animal
INTERSTITIAL CELL	A small rounded cell with clear cytoplasm and a relatively large nucleus containing one or two nucleoli
INTESTINE	The division of the digestive tract in which absorption takes place
JELLYFISH	Any of various marine free-swimming coelenterates having a more or less transparent body of a jellylike consistency
LARVA, *PL.* LARVAE	A young animal which has left the egg and is leading a free life, but which has not yet completed its development
LITHOCYST	A marginal sense-organ in campanularian medusae
LITTORAL	A region along the shore
MANUBRIUM	The extension of a medusa's body bearing the mouth
MEDUSA	A free-swimming jellyfish
MEDUSOID	The sexual generation of the Hydromedusae and Scyphomedusae
MESENTERY	One of the partitions in the body cavity of anthozoan coelenterates
MESOGLEA	Noncellular jellylike substance lying between the ectoderm and endoderm in the Coelenterata

METAGENESIS	The alternation of a sexual with an asexual generation in reproduction, in the life cycle of certain coelenterates
MUTUALISM	An association of two species which is beneficial to both of them
NECTOPHORE	A swimming bell
NEMATOCYST	One of the stinging organs in the coelenterates produced by a single cell, a cnidoblast
NEMATOPHORE	A small specialized defensive polyp, consisting of a hydrotheca and an elongated body armed with nematocysts
NEURON	A nerve cell
OPERCULUM	A plate closing an opening or covering some other structure
OVARY	The female sexual gland
OVUM	The female sexual cell, the egg
PALP	A projecting part or process, sensory in function, often near the mouth
PAPILLA	A small nipple-shaped elevation
PEDAL DISC	That part of the body in sea anemones which is either permanently or temporarily attached at one end
PEDALIUM	The base of a tentacle which is expanded to form a prominent flattened structure
PEDICEL	A small or short stalk or stem
PELAGIC	Of or inhabiting the open water, away from shore, as in the sea
PENETRANT	A large spherical nematocyst which is armed with three long spines and three spiral rows of small thorns on the base of the thread-tube, which lies, when at rest and undischarged, in transverse coils in the interior of the nematocyst
PERISARC	The cuticular outer covering of a hydroid

PERONIA	Thickenings of the ectoderm at the base of the tentacles in Narcomedusae
PHARYNX	The division of the alimentary canal immediately back of the mouth
PHYLUM	Any one of the main taxonomic divisions into which the animal kingdom is divided
PINNA	A feather or feather-like part
PINNATE	Shaped like a feather
PLANKTON	A collective term referring to all small forms of life in the surface waters of the sea or fresh water
PLANULA	The ciliated free-swimming larva of many coelenterates
POLYMORPHISM	The occurrence of several distinct forms in an animal species
POLYP	The form of a coelenterate having the shape of an elongated cylinder fastened at the aboral end, with the mouth and tentacles at the free oral end
RACHIS	The upper portion of the Pennatulacea containing the polyps
RADIAL CANAL	A certain canal in jellyfishes
RADIAL SYMMETRY	Having the parts or organs arranged symmetrically about a common center like the spokes of a wheel
REGENERATION	Replacement by growth of a part of the body that has been lost
REPRODUCTION	The production of an organism of others of its own kind
RESPIRATION	The processes by which an organism secures oxygen from the air or water, distributes it, combines it with substances in the tissues, and gives off carbon dioxide
RETRACTOR MUSCLE	The muscle which draws an organ towards its point of attachment
RHOPALIA	The sense organs or tentaculocysts of the scyphomedusans

ROOT-STALK	The hydrorhiza of a hydroid
SCYPHOSTOMA	The hydroid generation of the Scyphomedusae
SENSE RECEPTOR	A cell that is very sensitive to stimuli
SEPTUM	One of the radial calcareous plates of a stony coral
SESSILE	Attached, not free moving
SEXUAL	Reproduction through the agency of sex cells
SIPHONOGLYPH	A ciliated groove at one end of the mouth in the Anthozoa
SIPHONOZOOID	Rudimentary zooid through which water flows into the endodermal canals in the Pennatulacea
SPECIES	Groups of actually or potentially interbreeding natural populations resembling one another closely and reproductively isolated from other such groups
SPERM	A mature reproductive male cell
SPOROSAC	A sessile medusoid, one which remains attached to the parent hydroid
STATOCYST	Organ of equilibrium in animals
STIMULUS	A change in the external or internal environment of an animal that brings about a response
STOLON	A shoot from the base of an animal which gives rise to new individuals
STOMACH	A division of the digestive tract in which digestion takes place
STEROLINE GLUTINANT	A type of nematocyst which is oval or elliptical in form and discharges a straight unarmed thread-tube
STREPTOLINE GLUTINANT	A type of nematocyst which is cylindrical or oval in form, and which has a thread-tube that is provided with a spiral row of minute thorns along its length, which when discharged tends to coil

STROBILATION	The process of terminal budding
SUBGENITAL POCKET	A pocket in the subumbrella of many scyphomedusans
SUBUMBRELLA	The oral surface of a medusa
SYMBIOSIS	The living together of two dissimilar organisms for mutual benefit
TENTACLE	An elongated tactile organ
TENTACULOCYST	The sense organs of the Scyphozoa
TESTIS	The male sexual gland
THECA	The outer wall of the calcareous cup of a stony coral
TROPHOSOME	The hydroid stage of hydromedusans
TROPHOZOOID	The youthful stage of a fungoid coral
VELARIUM	The false velum of Cubomedusae
VELUM	The circular muscular locomotory membrane of a hydromedusan
VOLVENT	A small pyriform or spherical nematocyst containing a thick unarmed thread-tube which makes a single loop in the interior of the nematocyst
ZOOID	One of the members of a hydroid or siphonophore colony
ZOOPHYTE	An animal that looks somewhat like a plant, such as a coral or sea anemone

Bibliography

Arnold, Augusta F. *The Sea-beach at Ebb-tide.* New York: Dover Publications, Inc., 1965

Buchsbaum, Ralph M. *Animals without Backbones.* Chicago: University of Chicago Press, 1938.

Cromie, William J. *The Living World of the Sea.* Englewood Cliffs, N.J.: Prentice-Hall, Inc., 1966.

Crowder, William. *A Naturalist at the Seashore.* New York: The Century Company, 1928.

Hegner, Robert W., and Stiles, Karl A. *College Zoology*, 8th ed. New York: The Macmillan Company, 1959.

Miner, Roy Waldo. *Field Book of Seashore Life.* New York: G. P. Putnam's Sons, 1950.

Pratt, Henry Sherring. *A Manual of the Common Invertebrate Animals, Exclusive of Insects.* Philadelphia: P. Blakiston's Son and Co., Inc., 1935.

Spotte, Stephen H. *Secrets of the Deep.* New York: Charles Scribner's Sons, 1976.

Index

189

191

192

193